Best Easy Day Hikes
Conejo Valley

Help Us Keep This Guide Up to Date

Every effort has been made by the author and editors to make this guide as accurate and useful as possible. However, many things can change after a guide is published—trails are rerouted, regulations change, facilities come under new management, etc.

We would appreciate hearing from you concerning your experiences with this guide and how you feel it could be improved and kept up to date. While we may not be able to respond to all comments and suggestions, we'll take them to heart and we'll also make certain to share them with the author. Please send your comments and suggestions to the following address:

GPP
Reader Response/Editorial Department
P.O. Box 480
Guilford, CT 06437

Or you may e-mail us at:

editorial@GlobePequot.com

Thanks for your input, and happy trails!

Best Easy Day Hikes Series

Best Easy Day Hikes
Conejo Valley

Allen Riedel

FALCONGUIDES

GUILFORD, CONNECTICUT
HELENA, MONTANA

AN IMPRINT OF GLOBE PEQUOT PRESS

FALCONGUIDES®

TOPO! Explorer software and SuperQuad source maps courtesy of National Geographic Maps. For information about TOPO! Explorer, TOPO!, and Nat Geo Maps products, go to www.topo.com or www .natgeomaps.com.

Project editor: David Legere
Layout artist: Kevin Mak
Maps created by Mapping Specialists © Morris Book Publishing, LLC.

Library of Congress Cataloging-in-Publication Data is available on file.

ISBN 978-0-7627-5292-8

Printed in the United States of America

10 9 8 7 6 5 4 3 2 1

For Sierra, Makaila, and Michael

Contents

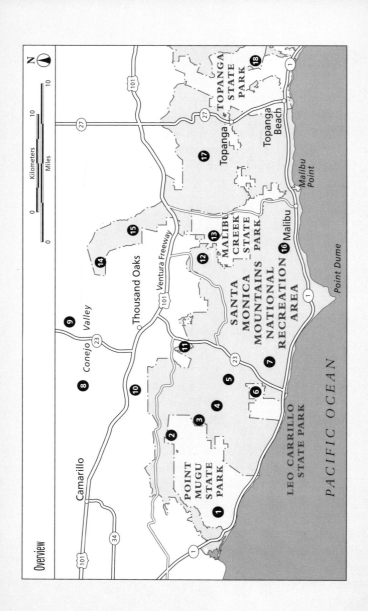

Acknowledgments

I would like to first and foremost thank all of the people who have spent time hiking with me in mountains, deserts, hills, forests, jungles, and on coastal beaches. Many of you, my friends, have inspired me in countless ways, and I can't thank you enough. I would like to mention some of you by name: Monique Riedel, Sean Coolican, Adam Mendelsohn, Michael Millenheft III, Sierra Riedel, Makaila Riedel, Tom Kashirsky, Cameron Alston, Matt Piazza, Bruno Lucidarme, Chrissy Ziburski, Eric Walther, Bob Romano, Jim Zuber, Danny Suarez, Dylan Riedel, Eric Romero, Donn DeBaun, Alex Wilson, Dawn Wilson, and Jane Weal.

I would also like to acknowledge my family: Monique, Michael, Sierra, and Makaila. All four of you have spent lots of time with me on trails that were great and some "not so much". . . . I love you with all my heart.

I also owe a lot to my mom and dad, Barbara and Elmer Riedel, who raised me to believe in myself. Thanks! Thanks to my brother, Larry; my grandparents, Herbert and Vivian Ward and Elmer and Lucille Riedel; and my in-laws, Anna and Richard Chavez. I am a better person because of all of you.

I am also grateful for the opportunities that I have been granted by writing for the most amazing website: www .localhikes.com. It seems Jim Zuber has been my biggest resource in the writing world, and I can never thank him enough for the awesome site and the amount of work he has sent my way. You rule, Jim!

I would like to thank Dave Ammenheuser and Patricia Mays at the *Press Enterprise,* who have been great editors and incredible to work for.

I would like to thank Scott Adams, John Burbidge and the wonderful people at Globe Pequot Press, as well as my other editors, Ashley, Kate, and Carol.

I would also like to thank Scott Ammons and all the terrific people at REI. It has been great getting started as an Outdoor School instructor.

Lastly, I would like to thank all of the students and teachers I have worked with over the past twelve years. It has been a joy knowing all of you.

Introduction

This book contains eighteen easy day hikes situated in and around the Conejo Valley region, with all eighteen being within a thirty-minute drive of the towns of Thousand Oaks, Westlake Village, Agoura, and Malibu. Surrounded by the Santa Monica Mountains, the area is rife with opportunities for hiking, with most being suitable for the entire family. The hikes are located in a variety of areas, ranging from national, state, county, city, and local parks to private lands. This book highlights the best short and easy hikes in the region.

Conejo in Spanish means rabbit. Undoubtedly due to the high concentrations of brush rabbits, jackrabbits, and desert cottontails in the region, Spanish explorers coming through the area in the late 1500s unceremoniously and perhaps not very creatively designated the area with a moniker that means "valley of the rabbits." Geographically, the valley abuts the San Fernando Valley on its eastern border. The Oxnard plain makes up the western edge, while the Simi Hills border the north. The entire southern border is graced by the lovely Santa Monica Mountains and the sparkling blue of the Pacific Ocean.

Open land is abundant throughout the region, with slices of parks, preserves, and reserves safeguarding some of the area's pastoral charm despite real estate's high value to land developers. The variety of scenery is quite diverse, providing many spectacular options for those looking to get outdoors and recreate. Parks, riparian woodlands, canyons, beaches, mountains, and verdant rolling hills are all a part of the landscape. Waterfalls, lakes, year-round creeks, volcanic outcroppings, and bluff hikes are all included in this book, but the opportunities for hiking in the area are almost limitless.

Resting just north of Los Angeles, the Conejo Valley is truly magnificent. At times it is difficult to believe that these open trails, hills, bluff sides, and coastal hikes are simply a stone's throw from one of the most populated urban areas in the world. One can hike in the Santa Monica Mountains without realizing or seeing any of the urbanization or industrialization of Los Angeles County.

Aside from the luscious coastline, the Santa Monica Mountains National Recreation Area is quite a treasure. The park is unique in that it is a conglomeration of federally owned land, state-run parks, local parks, and private landowners. All together the park contains more than 240 square miles. The park was established on November 10, 1978, and many parcels of land have been donated by celebrities that live in the surrounding Malibu region.

Weather along the coast of California is generally mild, though inland temperatures can be excruciatingly hot in the summer. Depending upon cloud cover and temperature, summer days can be pleasant or absolutely desiccating. Most summer hikes not directly on the coast are better suited to travel in the morning or evening hours. Weather patterns can and do shift, however, and the area can be socked in with fog any time of year. The farther inland you travel, less fog should be expected. Hiking and exercising in the region is popular throughout the day during the fall, winter, and spring. Spring is truly the best time to hike in the region for several reasons: The weather is generally agreeable, wildflowers are plentiful, water runs abundantly, including in the waterfalls, and the hillsides are green and lovely.

Mammals abound in the mountainous regions, with larger creatures such as mule deer, coyote, and mountain lions inhabiting the higher reaches. Not really presenting much of a danger, the habitat of these predators is not as threatened as in other areas of Southern California. Smaller creatures and rodents, such as squirrels, skunks, possums, mice, and of course rabbits, inhabit the upper and lower coastal regions. Many species of raptor can be seen along the coast and in mountain regions.

Nothing presents much of a danger to hikers except for the possibility of encountering rattlesnakes and spiders. Do not walk through tall grasses or place your hands and feet into locations unseen. Snakes are afraid of humans, and they understand the world through sensing vibrations. Typically, snakes will be alerted and flee long before a human approaches on the trail. Rattlesnakes will only strike if threatened, so the best thing to do is back away or walk in a wide berth around them on the trail.

Insects are not normally an issue in the region, though after rains ticks can present a problem, as can mosquitoes and other pests. Always check for ticks, for they can be present any time of the year, especially if you brush up against tall grasses. Flies and gnats can be slightly troublesome in wetter areas, but are not normally a nuisance. A mild insect repellent should do the trick for most hikes, and dogs should be protected with proper vaccinations and pet medicines.

Watch out for poison oak, with its three-pronged leaves. Poison oak is ubiquitous in the area and present on almost every trail. Its toxic oil, urushiol, is difficult to remove and can be spread if skin and clothing are not thoroughly cleansed after contact. Take care to avoid the plant.

Weather

The Conejo Valley mostly enjoys a semiarid Mediterranean climate, though coastal areas and the lower elevations can be pleasantly mild during the months of June, July, August, and September. Fog, wind, and cold can be a factor any time of year, so hikers should be prepared for quick changes in weather. Heat can also be an issue year-round, though late October through May are generally milder even in the hotter parts of the region.

Rain is not the normal state of affairs in Southern California, and the Conejo Valley is no exception, getting between 10 and 12 inches annually. The rainy season is typically from November through February, with showers more likely during December and January. Most rainstorms are over as quickly as they begin, though the region does see periods of continuing rainfall during the winter.

Summer temperatures can reach triple digits inland, though the coastal cities rarely rise above the 80s. The best times of year to hike in and around the Conejo Valley are fall through spring, when the temperatures are mild during the day. Early mornings, just before and after sunrise, and evenings, right before and after sunset, are pleasant in the summer almost anywhere in the area.

Preparing for Your Hike

Before you go hiking, always be prepared. Let someone know where you are planning to go, and leave an itinerary of your hiking destination with a reliable friend. Provide an expected return time and the name of the trailhead you are starting from, along with the specific route you will be taking. Be sure that your friend will contact authorities should you not return when expected.

Water is essential. Hydrate before you leave and during your hike, and leave extra water in your vehicle so you can hydrate upon return. A good rule of thumb is to drink one-half to one liter per hour of hiking, and on hot days without shade, you should drink as much as one gallon per hour of hiking. Salty snacks can help aid water retention. Avoid overexertion during the hottest part of the day.

When you hike, you should bring along the "Ten Essentials" to provide yourself with the basic necessities for survival should the unexpected occur:

1. Navigation (map, compass, GPS)
2. Sun protection (hat, sunscreen)
3. Insulation (layered clothing)
4. Illumination (head lamp, flashlight)
5. First-aid supplies (Band-Aids, bandages, gauze, tape, tweezers, etc.)
6. Repair kit and tools (knife, duct tape, etc.)
7. Nutrition (extra food)
8. Hydration (extra water)
9. Emergency shelter (tarp, tent, sleeping bag, or emergency blanket)
10. Fire starter (necessary for life-threatening emergencies only)

Hiking is a relatively safe activity, especially when care is taken, although it is always best to prepare for any eventuality. Minor mishaps, like taking a wrong turn, getting back after dark, or being lost for a short while, can be frightening, but as long as a cool head prevails, most outdoor situations can be easily rectified. The "Ten Essentials" are designed to keep people safe and provide a backup plan should something go wrong.

Other items may be fun to have along as well. Cameras can be used to record an excursion for posterity, while binoculars come in handy for wildlife viewing. Plant, bird, mammal, and insect identification guides can prove to be informative and educational. Handheld global positioning satellite (GPS) units are becoming more and more inexpensive and are a great tool to use on the trail. Maps should be taken, but most trails are well marked and maintained.

Clothing, Shoes, and Gear

Clothing should be made up of layers to protect your body from the elements, whether wind, heat, rain, or cold. An insulating layer of water- and sweat-wicking fabric (polyester, neoprene, Capilene®, or other synthetic fiber) is best for a basic layer. These fabrics wick sweat away from your body and keep you warm. On hot days cotton can be a good choice only because sweat will remain in the fabric, keeping you cooler than a synthetic material. Cotton is a bad choice for cold and rainy days, since the material retains water and loses its ability to insulate, which in extreme circumstances can lead to hypothermia.

A fleece shell is good for an insulating layer, because the material is lightweight and dries quickly. On days without a hint of precipitation, a fleece jacket may be the only outerwear needed.

Lastly, a lightweight rain shell should be brought along in case of emergencies. Rain and snow can be deadly in the mountains. A waterproof shell and pants offer protection from the elements.

Improvements in lightweight hiking boots and shoes over the past decade have revolutionized the sport. Boots no longer need to be bulky, heavy, cumbersome, Frankenstein-like appendages that cause blisters, chafing, and sore feet. Instead, many outdoor specialty shops can measure a hiker's feet and find a great-fitting shoe that can be worn immediately on the trail. These shoes are durable and sturdy and are excellent for short day hikes, though they may not be ideal for longer and more difficult trekking.

Socks made of wool or synthetic materials are best, as they pull moisture away from the feet, reducing chafing and blisters.

Backpacks for day hiking should be small, fit comfortably, and be capable of carrying ten to twenty pounds. Carrying more than twenty pounds on a day hike is actually kind of silly, and will probably only serve to make the experience less enjoyable. In today's ultralight market, weeklong backpacking trips can be made carrying only twenty to twenty-five pounds (water and food included), so find a backpack that is large enough to carry what is needed but light enough to be comfortable. Hydration systems have become the norm, and drinking from a reservoir through a tube is pure bliss compared to the days of cumbersome canteens or stopping to retrieve water bottles from a pack when thirsty.

Trail Regulations/Restrictions

Trails in this guide are located in national parks, state parks, preserves, and local and regional parks. Some trails pass through private property. As of this writing, access is allowed in private areas, but care should be taken not to abuse this privilege. Be careful and courteous, and always respect private property. Landowners can shut off access if unsightly trash and negative behavior becomes the norm. Do your part to protect these refuges.

Some city parks and natural areas are free, while others require day-use fees. Fees for trailhead usage are not required anywhere, though camping permits may carry fees.

Play It Safe

Generally, hiking in and around the Conejo Valley is a safe and fun way to explore the outdoors. Hiking is not without its risks, but there are ways to lessen those risks. Following a few simple steps and guidelines will help to make the activity as benign as possible:

- It is a good idea to know simple first aid, including how to treat bleeding, bites and stings, and fractures, strains, or sprains. Be sure to take along at least a basic first-aid kit. It won't help to have the skills without any supplies.

- Conejo Valley, and all of Southern California for that matter, is known for sunny skies and a warm climate. The sun can be powerful, especially at higher elevations. Use sunscreen and wear a wide-brimmed hat.

- Weather patterns can change abruptly. Carry the proper layers of clothing to protect you from temperature changes and rain.

- Rattlesnakes may be found on any of the hikes described, particularly from early spring to mid-fall. Be careful where you place your hands and feet.

- Learn how to spot and identify poison oak. Its appearance will change throughout the year. During spring and summer, the distinctive three-pronged leaf is green, and then turns to red and brown as the season progresses into winter. In winter, the leaves may completely fall off the plant, leaving a hard-to-identify stalk that still contains and spreads its toxic oil when touched. The noxious plant grows abundantly near water, in canyons, and along hillsides.

- Ticks are another pest to be avoided. They are more likely to be found near water or after rains, and hang in the brush waiting to drop on warm-blooded animals. It is a good idea to check for ticks whenever you pause along the trail. Ticks will generally hang on to clothing or hair and don't bite until the host has stopped moving. Remove them before they have a chance to bite.

Etiquette

There really aren't any rules for hiking, other than those outlined by specific parks and agencies that govern each parcel of land, but there are a few unwritten guidelines to follow. Mostly they are common sense, but some are not always intuitive. Right of way on the trail is always as follows: equestrians first, pedestrians next, and then bicyclists. Hikers and bicyclists must always yield to horses, and bicyclists must always yield to hikers.

While it isn't necessarily written, the courteous thing to do on the trail is to always yield to uphill hikers. Hiking uphill is harder and more taxing; when walking uphill hikers get into a rhythm, and making them stop is just plain rude. However, those hiking uphill will often stop to let downhill hikers pass simply to get a rest. If you are hiking downhill and you notice the people coming your way have some serious mojo going, let them continue. It is a lot easier getting started going down. Of course, common sense should also rule the day. Backpackers carrying heavy loads on narrow trails might need hikers going uphill to step aside, and equestrian users may find a suitable space to stop before a hiker even comes close to them.

When hiking with dogs, always bring a leash. Even if there is no requirement that a dog be leashed, some people are afraid of dogs and it is courteous to leash dogs up when others approach. Unruly and vicious dogs are better left at home, as dog owners are legally liable for any damage their pets may cause. Make sure your pet is trained when off leash so that it will not disturb or harass wildlife or others.

Zero Impact

Trails in the Conejo Valley area are used year-round. We, as trail users and advocates, must be especially vigilant to make sure our passage leaves no lasting mark. Here are some basic guidelines for preserving trails in the region:

- Pack out all your own trash, including biodegradable items like orange peels and sunflower seeds. In the arid Southern California climate, items such as these take ten or more years to decompose. If everyone who hiked these trails left peels and shells behind, the trails would look more like a waste dump than a forest or wild landscape. You might also pack out garbage left by less considerate hikers—take a plastic bag and make the place better for your having been there.

- Don't approach or feed any wild creatures—the ground squirrel eyeing your snack food is best able to survive if it remains self-reliant.
- Don't pick wildflowers or gather rocks, antlers, feathers, or other treasures along the trail. Removing these items will only take away from the next hiker's experience.
- Avoid damaging trailside soils and plants by remaining on the established route. This is also a good rule of thumb for avoiding poison oak and stinging nettle, common regional trailside irritants.
- Don't cut switchbacks, which can promote erosion.
- Be courteous by not making loud noises while hiking.
- Many of these trails are multiuse, which means you'll share them with other hikers, trail runners, mountain bikers, and equestrians. Familiarize yourself with the proper trail etiquette, yielding the trail when appropriate.
- Use outhouses at trailheads or along the trail.
- Be respectful of private property rights.

The Falcon Zero-Impact Principles
- Leave with everything you brought with you.
- Leave no sign of your visit.
- Leave the landscape as you found it.

How to Use This Guide

This guide is designed to be simple and easy to use. Each hike is described with a map and summary information that delivers the trail's vital statistics including distance, approximate hiking time, elevation gain, difficulty, trail surface, best season, other trail users, canine compatibility, fees and permits, and trail contacts. Directions to the trailhead are also provided, along with a general description of what you'll see along the way. A detailed route finder (Miles and Directions) sets forth mileages between significant landmarks along the trail.

Maps

Easy to follow maps are provided for each hike. All the hikes in this book are covered by Topo! CD: California CD 9, National Parks CD 5, Pacific State and the Far West, and the detailed topographic maps published by the U.S. Geological Survey (USGS).

Hike Selection

The hikes listed in this book range from leisurely strolls to more challenging hikes. You will find hikes that range in distance from about 1 mile to 7 miles, across varying terrain. Whether you are visiting for a weekend, or a local of many years, you should find a hike in this book to serve your interests. There are excellent options for getting a good workout, as well as options that are best for days when you just want to get outside without too much effort. It is important to remember that while we believe these are the best easy day hikes in the area, not every hike is right for every person. Be sure to check out the trail finder to help you choose the right hike for you and your hiking partners.

Dividing the Conejo Valley

The trails covered in this book can be broken into two distinct parts: the Santa Monica Mountains National Recreation Area (hikes 1–7 and 12–18) and the Conejo Open Space Trails (hikes 8–11).

Santa Monica Mountains National Recreation Area

Part of the Transverse Ranges of Southern California, the Santa Monica Mountains run west to east from Point Mugu to Griffith Park. They are rimmed on the north by the Conejo and San Fernando Valleys, and to the south they are entirely bounded by the Pacific Ocean. Located in southeast Ventura County and western Los Angeles County, the mountains span 40 miles from end to end and are bisected by several roads and highways. The Santa Monica Mountains National Recreation Area (SMMNRA) is the world's largest urban national park. At nearly 240 square miles, the park supports a whopping twenty-six different zip codes and five separate area codes.

Established on November 10, 1978, the Santa Monica Mountains National Recreation Area has been a beneficiary of land donations, private and public acquisitions, concerned citizens, generous donors, activists, and celebrity benefactors. To this day the Santa Monica Mountains Conservancy is working to buy back, preserve, protect, and restore the land in the region for public access and wildlife habitat. The recreation area is made up of a conglomeration of nationally operated sites (headquartered in Thousand Oaks), state parks, regional and local parks, and private lands, with over seventy different parks and open spaces included.

Historically, the Santa Monica Mountains were home to the Chumash, Tataviam, and Gabrielino/Tongva peoples. The Santa Monicas formed an overlap in the three cultures' territory. The 1542 arrival of explorer Juan Rodriguez Cabrillo brought the Spanish, Catholicism, the mission culture, and non-native plants to the region, forever changing the landscape and ushering in the modernization and urbanization that continues today.

Despite being adjacent to the world's eleventh largest metropolitan area, much of the Santa Monica Range has been protected. There are places that feel so remote it is difficult to believe the park is located in Los Angeles. It is quite possible that many of the canyons, ridgelines, and plateaus look nearly unchanged from the days of the Native Americans.

For more information, check out Santa Monica Mountains National Recreation Area; 401 West Hillcrest Drive, Thousand Oaks, CA 91360; (805) 370-2301; www.nps .gov/samo.

Conejo Open Space Trails

The Conejo Open Space Conservation Agency (COSCA) is an agency created in 1977 between the City of Thousand Oaks and the Conejo Recreation and Parks District to conserve open lands in an undeveloped state. Their website (http://conejo-openspace.org/index.htm) states their goal as: "By providing a refuge from urbanization for both people and wildlife, the open space system is an investment in the future. Unlike so many things in today's world, this is a resource which appreciates in value for both people and wildlife as the years go by. Hopefully, with your help, our open space system will continue to offer a safe, stable environment for all organisms, whose complex interactions combine to form viable ecosystems."

Currently the agency manages 11,300 acres of open space, which includes over 140 miles of trails and includes over 38 individual parks and management areas. The Conejo Open Space Foundation is a non-profit organization committed to promoting, educating, maintaining, and protecting the open spaces (www.cosf.org). The parks and open spaces of the Conejo Valley act as a buffer and extension of the Santa Monica Mountains National Recreation Area, providing species habitat and interlinking trails for human usage. The parks range in size and usage, but offer some amazing hiking trails, including those that have great viewpoints, spectacular waterfalls, and wonderful woodlands.

Difficulty Ratings

These are all easy hikes, but easy is a relative term. A fit runner may find a 3-mile, hilly hike easy, while some may expect easy to be short and flat. First time hikers and seasoned veterans likely also have different expectations. So to aid in the selection of a hike that suits your particular needs and abilities, each hike is rated easy, moderate, or more challenging. Bear in mind that even the most challenging routes can be made easy by hiking within your limits and taking rests when you need them.

- **Easy** hikes are generally short and/or have little elevation gain, usually taking no more than an hour to complete.

- **Moderate** hikes involve more elevation gain, and may require slightly more coordination than the easy hikes, often crossing streams or scrambling over rocks.
- **More challenging** hikes feature some steep stretches, greater distances, and generally require more fitness and technical skills.

These are completely subjective ratings—consider that what you think is easy is entirely dependent on your level of fitness and coordination, and the adequacy of your gear. If you are hiking with a group, you should select a hike with a rating that's appropriate for the least fit and prepared in your party.

Approximate hiking times are based on the assumption that on flat ground, most walkers average 2 to 3 miles per hour. Adjust that rate by the steepness of the terrain and your level of fitness (subtract time if you're an aerobic animal and add time if you're hiking with kids), and you have a ballpark hiking duration. Be sure to add more time if you plan to picnic or take part in other activities like bird watching or photography. It is also important to note that a hiking trip does not only entail moving time. Plan more time if you tend to take a lot of pictures, or stop to frequently take in views.

Trail Finder

Best Hikes for Children

Best Hikes for Waterfalls

Best Hikes for Views

Best Hikes for Nature

Map Legend

══⟨101⟩══	U.S. Highway
══⟨23⟩══	State Highway
═══════	Local Road
= = = = = =	Unpaved Road
▬▬▬▬▬▬	Featured Trail
- - - - - - -	Trail
⌐ ⎯ ⎯ ⎯	Intermittent Stream
⬭	Body of Water
▭ ▭	Local/State Park
▭ ▭	National Recreation Area
‿	Bridge
▲	Campground
⸸	Gate
▲	Mountain/Peak
🅿	Parking
🏕	Picnic Area
■	Point of Interest/Structure
🏠	Ranger Station
○	Town
⓫	Trailhead
🔍	Viewpoint/Overlook
❓	Visitor Center/Information
≋	Waterfall

1 La Jolla Loop

Walk through peaceful riparian canyons and an incredible valley surrounded by the beauty of the Santa Monica Mountains.

Distance: 5.5-mile lollipop
Approximate hiking time: 3 hours
Elevation gain: 1,200 feet
Difficulty: Moderate
Trail surface: Dirt, rock
Best season: Year-round; spring for wildflowers and water; hot in summer
Other trail users: Equestrians
Canine compatibility: Dogs not permitted

Fees and permits: A day use/parking fee is charged.
Trail contact: Point Mugu State Park, 9000 West Pacific Coast Hwy., Malibu, CA 90265; (818) 880-0363; www.parks.ca.gov/?page_id=630. Santa Monica Mountains National Recreation Area, 401 West Hillcrest Dr., Thousand Oaks, CA 91360; (805) 370-2301; www.nps.gov/samo

Finding the trailhead: From the intersection of US 101 and Lindero Canyon Road in Westlake Village, take US 101 north/west for 1 mile. Take exit 40 for Westlake Boulevard/CA 23. Turn left onto South Westlake Boulevard. Drive for 5.4 miles. At the intersection with Mulholland Highway/CA 23 turn right onto Mulholland Highway/CA 23 and drive for 12 miles, following the signs for CA 23 to the Pacific Coast Highway (CA 1). Turn right onto CA 1/Pacific Coast Highway and drive for 7.3 miles. Turn right and park in the Point Mugu State Park parking lot. GPS Trailhead Coordinates: 34° 05' 12" N, -119° 02' 13" W

The Hike

Walk to the north end of the parking area to the signed trailhead for La Jolla Canyon Trail. The trail climbs up through the wild canyon gently for the first 0.25 mile. A brief steep section follows and lasts for a little over 0.25 mile; at that point the trail eases up and the climb remains gentle for the remainder of the uphill section. Right in the middle of the steep section, especially after rains, there is a fabulous waterfall that pours over moss, grass, and rocks. It quickly turns to a trickle and then a drip when the rainy season dries up. The canyon however, remains ripe and lovely, with the walls rising up above the trail in the shape of a V. The slender canyon trail meanders above the creek, where oak and sycamore line the riparian ecosystem.

At just over the 1-mile mark, the trail comes to a junction with the La Jolla Loop Trail. Turn right and head north along the trail that lingers in the canyon. Follow the loop through the canyon until you reach a pond at 1.6 miles. Turn left onto the La Jolla Canyon Loop Trail, the loop is clearly marked at all points.

The trail begins to open up and look into La Jolla Valley, a wonderful meadow situated on a high plateau. The mountains ring the valley in nearly a perfect circle. Views of the ridgeline of the sacred Chumash peaks—Boney Mountain, Mugu Peak, La Jolla Peak, and Laguna Peak—are spectacular. If timed right for late winter/early spring, an abundance of blossoming wildflowers carpets the meadow. If cool breezes persist, the area feels more than a little bit like paradise.

At 2.25 miles the trail crosses a more sparingly used bisector trail that bisects the valley and loop. Continue

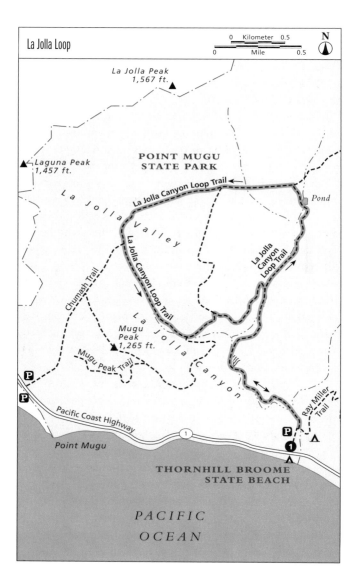

La Jolla Loop

0   Kilometer 0.5

0   Mile   0.5

N

La Jolla Peak
1,567 ft.

Laguna Peak
1,457 ft.

POINT MUGU
STATE PARK

La Jolla Valley

La Jolla Canyon Loop Trail

Pond

Chumash Trail

La Jolla Canyon Loop Trail

La Jolla Canyon Loop Trail

Mugu
Peak
1,265 ft.

La Jolla Canyon

Mugu Peak Trail

Ray Miller Trail

P
P

Pacific Coast Highway

Point Mugu

1

P
1

THORNHILL BROOME
STATE BEACH

PACIFIC
OCEAN

straight and follow the loop. In less than 0.1 mile the route reaches its high point and the remainder of the hike is a downhill venture. At 3 miles, the route meets the Chumash Trail, a 7,000-year-old trail used by the Native Americans who once called the region home. Using this route, they climbed straight up and down in a no-nonsense fashion between coastal tide pools and this valley, which was once home to a sprawling village. The Spanish explorer Juan Rodriguez Cabrillo made note of the village at Point Mugu in his expedition logs. It isn't hard to imagine the wonderful scene in this valley, because the grandeur remains.

Those with enough energy and gumption may want to add 1 mile and 500 feet of elevation gain to the round-trip total and hike to the top of Mugu Peak before returning to the trailhead. Otherwise, ignore the Mugu Peak loop, which is on the right at 3.6 miles.

At 3.9 miles the trail again intersects with the valley bisector trail. Soon after, incredible views of the ocean appear through the canyon. At 4.5 miles, turn right at the junction with the outgoing leg of the loop, and descend back down La Jolla Canyon to the trailhead. *La jolla* means "the jewel" in Spanish. After hiking here, there can be no wonder at that designation.

Miles and Directions

0.0 From the parking area, walk north to the trailhead.

0.65 Look for the waterfall on the left of the trail.

1.0 Take the right fork and continue on the La Jolla Loop Trail.

1.6 Reach the pond, turn left at the junction, and follow the trail on the western side of the pond.

1.8 Stay left at the junction and continue on the La Jolla Loop.

2.25 Continue straight at the intersection with the unmarked valley bisector trail.

3.0 Stay left at the junction with the Chumash Trail.

3.6 Stay left at the junction with the Mugu Peak Trail.

3.9 Stay right at the unsigned valley bisector trail.

4.5 Turn right onto the La Jolla Canyon Trail that leads back to the parking lot.

5.5 Arrive back in the parking area.

2 Satwiwa and Old Boney Waterfall Trails

Take a hike through lovely Satwiwa and Point Mugu State Park to a cascading waterfall.

Distance: 3.5-mile loop
Approximate hiking time: 2 hours
Elevation gain: 500 feet
Difficulty: Easy
Trail surface: Dirt and sand, creek crossings
Best season: Year-round; spring for water and wildflowers; hot in summer
Other trail users: None
Canine compatibility: Leashed dogs permitted in Satwiwa/Rancho Sierra Vista but no dogs are allowed in Point Mugu State Park.

Fees and permits: None
Trail contact: Satwiwa/Rancho Sierra Vista, 4126 W Potrero Rd., Newbury Park, CA 91320; (805) 375-1930; www.nps .gov/samo/planyourvisit/ rsvsatwiwa.htm. Point Mugu State Park, 9000 West Pacific Coast Hwy., Malibu, CA 90265; (818) 880-0363; www.parks .ca.gov/?page_id=630. Santa Monica Mountains National Recreation Area, 401 West Hillcrest Dr., Thousand Oaks, CA 91360; (805) 370-2301; www.nps.gov/ samo

Finding the trailhead: From the intersection of US 101 and Lindero Canyon Road in Westlake Village, drive northwest on US 101 for 6.3 miles. Take exit 47B for Borchard Road. Turn right onto Borchard Road. Drive for 1.8 miles. Turn left onto Reino Road. Drive for 1.4 miles and make a slight right onto West Potrero Road. Continue for 0.5 miles. Take the second left onto Potrero Road. Follow it for 0.4 mile to the parking lot at the end of the road. GPS Trailhead Coordinates: 34° 09' 10" N, -118° 57' 55" W

The Hike

The trail begins by heading east from the east end of the Satwiwa/Rancho Sierra Vista parking lot near the restroom. The trail joins up with Potrero Road, also called the Ranch Overlook Trail (closed to non-authorized vehicles), and travels through a lovely tree-lined creekbed. At 0.3 mile the road intersects with several trails. Turn left and cross the first footbridge. Immediately, before the second footbridge, turn right onto the unmarked Satwiwa Loop Trail. The trail climbs a little and at 0.5 mile meanders next to a marshy swampland replete with sounds of insects and frogs. It is not unusual to see wildlife here, from deer to coyote to roadrunners to raptors: Keep an open eye on the surroundings especially in the morning. Views of the looming Boney Mountain ridgeline leave no wonder as to why the Chumash inhabitants of the region once believed that the mountain was the sacred home of all creation.

Once on the Satwiwa Loop Trail, several side trails will intersect the path but should be avoided. Continue straight until the only option, at 0.75 mile, is to turn left onto the old Danielson Road. Hike up the road until the signed Y intersection for the waterfall trail at 0.87 mile. Turn right and begin descending the Old Boney Trail. At 1.25 miles the road makes a hairpin turn. Here the main trail curves around farther into Point Mugu State Park and the side trail to the waterfall continues straight. There are signs, so the way is very clear.

The trail starts up again, heading upstream along the creek. The route becomes a much smaller trail and can become overgrown in spots. There are a few water crossings, which are not very difficult unless there is a lot of runoff present during the rainy season. At 1.5 miles the trail seems to end, but continuing to the right, over one more creek crossing and through some rocks, will lead to the quaint 40-foot series of cascades.

When ready to return, head back up to Danielson Road, at 2.15 miles. Turn right to continue along the Satwiwa Loop Trail. In 0.1 mile, turn left and continue on the smaller but still wide trail, heading north along the Satwiwa Loop. Continue straight to the windmill, ignoring all intersecting smaller use trails. Take the left trail at the windmill and follow it through a grassy plateau back along the pond and marshland to the Satwiwa Native American Cultural Center and a Chumash demonstration village where a model Chumash home, called an *ap,* is exhibited in various stages of construction. A Native American guest host or park ranger is on hand to answer questions from 9 a.m. to 5 p.m. on weekends.

From the village, continue straight and cross both footbridges. Turn right onto the road (the Ranch Overlook Trail), and return to the parking lot.

Miles and Directions

- **0.0** The trail begins just to the right of the restroom in the parking lot.
- **0.2** The trail joins Potrero Road (Ranch Overlook Trail).
- **0.3** Take the left trail and cross the first footbridge. Take the trail on the right immediately after the footbridge.
- **0.75** At the end of the trail, turn left onto Danielson Road.
- **0.87** At the Y intersection, turn right and take the Old Boney Trail.
- **1.25** At the bottom of the gorge, continue straight on the trail.
- **1.4** Old Boney Road hairpins; continue straight on the trail to the waterfall.

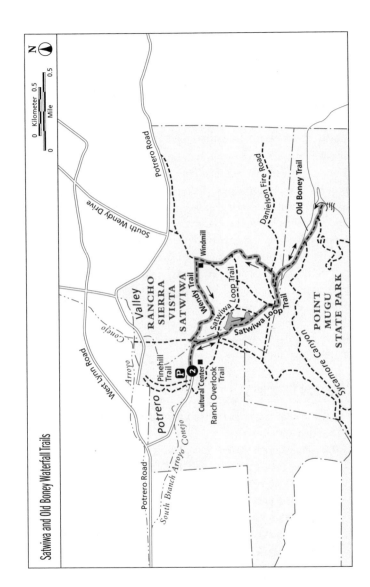

Satwiwa and Old Boney Waterfall Trails

1.5 Reach the waterfall. Return via Old Boney Road to the junction with Danielson Road.

2.15 Turn right onto Danielson Road.

2.25 Turn left onto the Satwiwa Loop Trail.

2.6 Take the left trail at the windmill.

3.2 Cross both footbridges and turn left.

3.5 Arrive back at the parking area.

3 Boney Mountain-Backbone Trail

Climb to the top of the tallest peak in the Santa Monica Mountains and wander below the volcanic spires of Boney Mountain.

Distance: 5 miles out and back
Approximate hiking time: 2.5 hours
Elevation gain: 1,100 feet
Difficulty: Moderate
Trail surface: Dirt and sand
Best season: Year-round, hot in summer
Other trail users: Equestrians

Canine compatibility: Leashed dogs permitted
Fees and permits: None
Trail contact: Circle X Ranch, 12896 Yerba Buena Rd., Malibu, CA 90265. Santa Monica Mountains National Recreation Area, 401 West Hillcrest Dr., Thousand Oaks, CA 91360; (805) 370-2301; www.nps.gov/samo

Finding the trailhead: From the intersection of US 101 and Lindero Canyon Road in Westlake Village, take US 101 northwest to exit 40 for CA 23 south. Turn left onto Westlake Boulevard/CA 23. Drive for 7.7 miles on CA 23, adhering to the signs. Turn right onto Little Sycamore Canyon, following Little Sycamore Canyon Road. Drive for 1.9 miles. Turn left onto Yerba Buena Road and drive for 2.7 miles, following the signs for Yerba Buena Road. Turn right into the dirt parking area for the trailhead. The trail leads up the old fire road beyond the locked gate and trailhead information sign. GPS Trailhead Coordinates: 34° 06' 42" N, -118° 55' 36" W

The Hike

This route bypasses the Mishe Mokwa Trail and instead focuses on the peaks of the Boney Mountain ridge and Mount Allen (Sandstone Peak), the highest summit in the

Santa Monica Mountains. From the parking area, walk north along the trail as it winds around the mountainside. The trail makes for a solid workout as it gains 1,000 feet in 1 mile. From that point, the walk is a relative breeze.

The trail is easy to follow as it's an old road. At 0.25 mile the Mishe Mokwa Trail intersects on the right. A beautiful trail in its own right (though not described here), it can be used as a loop on the way in or on the way out. It is longer and gains elevation less steeply than the Backbone Trail. Continue straight and to the left on the Backbone, winding around to the north side of the mountain.

At 1 mile, a short spur trail on the left leads to the top of Mount Allen, also known as Sandstone Peak. Climb to the top. At 3,111 feet it is the tallest thing around, and the views are truly sensational. The wide Pacific can be seen shimmering to the south, as can a wide swath of the Malibu community. On clear days, five of the Channel Islands can clearly be seen from the summit. The spiny ridge of Boney Mountain hovers on the horizon to the north.

From the top of Mount Allen, return to the trail, turn left, and continue hiking along the road. Here the trail loses some elevation and enters into a strange and eerie valley. The entire region looks like a land out of time, and it is hard to shake the feeling that dinosaurs or some sort of aliens from a low-budget science fiction movie might be lurking right around the corner. The spires and rock outcroppings are made up of andesite breccia, which is a volcanic and sedimentary rock. The rock was uncovered by uplifting and tectonic forces. None of it is sandstone, although it does resemble it.

At 1.8 miles, a very short spur on the left leads off the main trail to Inspiration Point, a worthy side jaunt. A marker

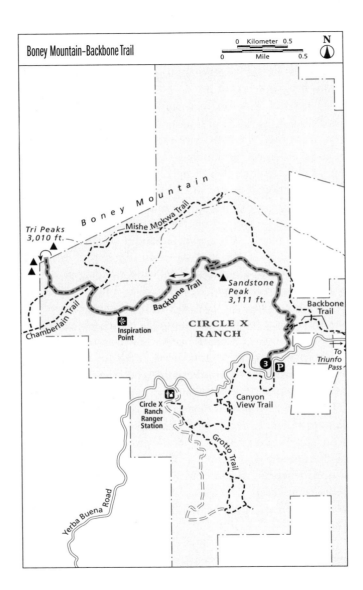

Boney Mountain-Backbone Trail

0   Kilometer   0.5

0   Mile   0.5

N

Boney Mountain

Tri Peaks
3,010 ft.

Mishe Mokwa Trail

Chamberlain Trail

Backbone Trail

Sandstone
Peak
3,111 ft.

Backbone
Trail

Inspiration
Point

CIRCLE X
RANCH

To
Triunfo
Pass

3

P

Circle X
Ranch
Ranger
Station

Canyon
View Trail

Grotto Trail

Yerba Buena Road

points out various Southern California peaks and landmarks. After taking in the sights, continue along the main trail to the connector with the western side of the Mishe Mokwa Trail. Here, many side trails and use trails enter the main trail. It is best to continue straight and head toward the Tri Peaks. They should be obvious on the skyline. Those who wish to bushwhack and scramble can climb up some rocks. Otherwise, take in the views and return via the same route.

Miles and Directions

0.0   Walk north from the parking area along the trail (actually an old road).

0.25 Continue straight and to the left at the junction with the Mishe Mokwa Trail.

1.0   Take the short spur on the left to the top of Mount Allen (Sandstone Peak).

1.8   Take the short spur on the left to Inspiration Point.

2.1   Continue straight at the junction with the Mishe Mokwa Trail. Keep straight on the trail, ignoring side spurs towards Tri Peaks along Boney Mountain ridge.

2.5   Arrive at the base of Tri Peaks along Boney Mountain ridge. Return via the same route.

5.0   Arrive back at the trailhead.

4 The Grotto

Descend into a lush and lovely canyon replete with flowing stream, wildflowers, and peaceful scenery.

Distance: 2.5 miles out and back
Approximate hiking time: 1.5 hours
Elevation gain: 400 feet
Difficulty: Easy
Trail surface: Dirt, creek crossings
Best season: Year-round; spring for water and wildflowers
Other trail users: None

Canine compatibility: Leashed dogs permitted
Fees and permits: None
Trail contact: Circle X Ranch, 12896 Yerba Buena Rd., Malibu, CA 90265; www.nps.gov/ samo/planyourvisit/circlexranch .htm. Santa Monica Mountains National Recreation Area, 401 West Hillcrest Dr., Thousand Oaks, CA 91360; (805) 370-2301; www.nps.gov/samo

Finding the trailhead: From the intersection of US 101 and Lindero Canyon Road in Westlake Village, take US 101 northwest to exit 40 for CA 23 south. Turn left onto Westlake Boulevard/CA 23. Drive for 7.7 miles on CA 23, adhering to the signs. Turn right on Little Sycamore Canyon Road. Drive for 1.9 miles. Turn left onto Yerba Buena Road and drive for 3.7 miles, following the signs for Yerba Buena Road. Turn left onto the unnamed signed entrance road to Circle X Ranch and follow it to the parking area. GPS Trailhead Coordinates: 34° 06' 29" N, -118° 56' 11" W

The Hike

The Grotto is a lovely slice of idyllic splendor sandwiched between ever narrowing canyon walls. The hike begins by leaving the parking area and meandering along the west fork of Arroyo Sequit. For a good portion of the route there is shade, though there are some exposed sections. If timed right, the canyon provides a majestic backdrop for winter rains. Multiple waterfalls can be seen along the route, as long as there is a lot of water. Of course, the drier it is, the more likely the falls are to dry up and simply be a trickle—if even that.

The hike heads south from the parking area and group campground. It is well signed and the path is easy to follow. Some creek crossings do occur, but these are all fairly easy to handle and should not present much of a problem, if any. Follow the trail and enjoy the scenery.

Within a couple of minutes, the trail crosses the creek just above and right next to the waterfall and meets a junction with the Canyon View Trail. Continue straight and leave the Canyon View Trail for another day. The trail opens up into a lovely meadow where views of distant craggy peaks are quite breathtaking. The trail is quiet and peaceful, but is frequently used. If there is ample water flowing in the creek, watch for other telltale signs of water across the canyon. More than one fall can be seen from this section of the trail.

From the meadow the trail drops again and crosses the creek two more times. At this point the Grotto is very near. It is easy to tell, as the walls of the canyon narrow and sedimentary stone towers seem to guard either side of the gorge. The water pours over the edge, and those who are fleet of foot will want to scramble down among the boulders and witness the peaceful waterfall. It is always flowing due to a spring that empties into the creek from the west.

Explore the open caverns and look in the pools for signs of amphibious wildlife. Newts and salamanders live here.

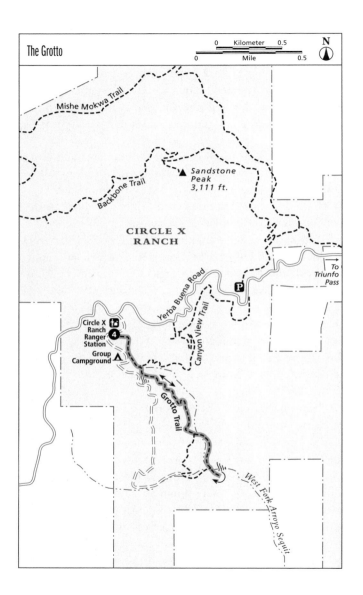

Please be cautious and only observe them: The pools they live in are closed ecosystems. Simply touching the water can spread bacteria and germs that could potentially extinguish the species in this region. One person touching the water may not seem harmful, but if five visitors a day spread germs and bacteria into the pools, it won't take very long to do irreparable damage. Please leave only footprints.

Return via the same route.

Miles and Directions

0.0 From the group campground, head south along the trail.

0.25 Continue straight at the junction with the Canyon View Trail.

1.25 Arrive at the Grotto. Return via same route.

2.5 Arrive back at the trailhead.

5 Arroyo Sequit

Hike along a secluded and lovely interactive canyon loop.

Distance: 1.75-mile lollipop
Approximate hiking time: 1 hour
Elevation gain: 325 feet
Difficulty: Easy
Trail surface: Sand, dirt, asphalt
Best season: Year-round; spring for water and wildflowers
Other trail users: Bicyclists, equestrians
Canine compatibility: Leashed dogs permitted

Fees and permits: None
Trail contact: Arroyo Sequit, 34138 Mulholland Hwy., Malibu, CA 90265; www.nps.gov/ samo/planyourvisit/arroyosequit .htm. Santa Monica Mountains National Recreation Area, 401 West Hillcrest Dr., Thousand Oaks, CA 91360; (805) 370- 2301; www.nps.gov/samo/.

Finding the trailhead: From the intersection of US 101 and Lindero Canyon Road in Westlake Village, take US 101 northwest for 1 mile. Take exit 40 for Westlake Boulevard/CA 23. Turn left onto South Westlake Boulevard/CA 23. Drive for 5.3 miles. Turn slightly right onto CA 23 S/Mulholland Highway, and drive for 3.5 miles, following the signs for CA 23. Turn left onto unsigned and unmarked Mason Road. Park in the Arroyo Sequit Park lot. GPS Trailhead Coordinates: 34° 05' 20" N, -118° 53' 26" W

The Hike

Arroyo Sequit is a tranquil slice of the Santa Monica Mountains, encompassing 320 acres of the coastal range. On first glance at a trail map, or the map of the Santa Monica Mountains National Recreation Area, the park seems little more than a dot along Mulholland Highway. Most people drive by and hardly notice. Since there isn't a sign driving northbound on Mulholland from the Pacific Coast Highway (PCH), some people trying to stop might actually miss the park and simply keep driving to seemingly grander destinations. That would be a mistake, as the simplicity of Arroyo Sequit is part of its beauty. The loop trail serves as a perfect introduction to one of the lovelier parcels of protected land in the region.

From the parking area, hike south along Mason Road. The route follows the asphalt for 0.2 mile before reaching the ranger residence. Bear left at the residence and hike along the road as it becomes gravel, and then dirt. Signs point the way to the nature trail.

The nature loop trail climbs along the hillside, granting generous views into the surrounding mountains. There are some houses with large lots nearby, which does detract somewhat from the natural beauty, but many people will find enjoyment wondering about the employment status and wealth of those who make their residence in such a beautiful landscape.

At 0.75 mile the trail stops climbing and descends into the canyon. Views to the large telescopes across the canyon and beyond open up for a little while, before the trail heads into the riparian gorge. A perennial stream runs through the gorge and keeps the surrounding countryside green and lush. The creek can be rather wild, and parts of the trail get washed away during winter rains and with runoff. Creek crossings also become slightly more labor intensive. Several crossings will have to be made.

The trail loops around, winding through the creek drainage and passing a beautiful but very seasonal waterfall. At 1.4 miles it climbs back up to the meadow near the ranger residence, and then meets back up with the road. Turn left and return to the parking area.

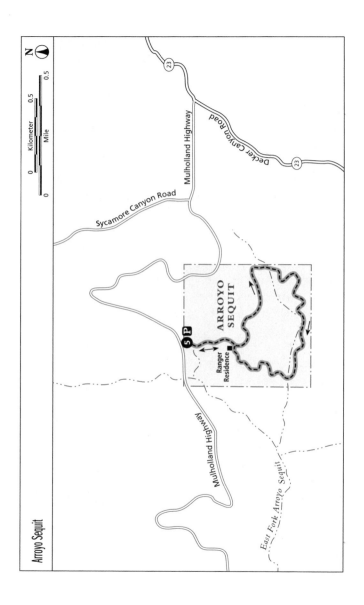

Arroyo Sequit

Chances are good that there won't be too many people on the trail. The park isn't quite as frequented as other spots in the Santa Monicas.

Miles and Directions

0.0 From the parking area, walk south along the road.

0.2 Turn left and follow the road until it turns into a trail.

0.3 Turn right onto the signed nature trail where it branches from the road, following the loop.

1.2 Stay right at the fork and follow the trail back to the meadow.

1.4 Reach the meadow near the ranger residence.

1.55 Turn left onto the road.

1.75 Arrive back at the trailhead and parking area.

6 Nicholas Flat

Hike in the upper reaches of Leo Carrillo State Park, through beautiful meadows, and take in heavenly views of the mountains and coast.

Distance: 2.6 miles out and back

Approximate hiking time: 1.5 hours

Elevation gain: 400 feet

Difficulty: Easy

Trail surface: Dirt

Best season: Year-round; spring for water and wildflowers

Other trail users: None

Canine compatibility: Dogs not permitted

Fees and permits: None

Trail contact: Leo Carrillo State Park, 35000 West Pacific Coast Hwy., Malibu, CA 90265; (310) 457-8143; www.parks .ca.gov/?page_id=616. Santa Monica Mountains National Recreation Area, 401 West Hillcrest Dr., Thousand Oaks, CA 91360; (805) 370-2301; www.nps.gov/ samo/

Finding the trailhead: From the intersection of US 101 and Lindero Canyon Road in Westlake Village, take US 101 northwest for 1 mile. Take exit 40 for Westlake Boulevard/CA 23. Turn left onto South Westlake Boulevard/CA 23. Drive for 5.4 miles. Veer slightly right onto Mulholland Highway/CA 23 and drive for 0.2 miles, turning slightly left to stay on Mulholland Highway/Decker Canyon Road/CA 23 for 3.9 miles. Follow the signs for CA 23. (At 1.7 miles Mulholland Highway/CA 23 becomes Decker Canyon Road, continue on the CA 23 for 2.2 miles.) Turn right onto Decker School Road, and drive for 1.2 miles. Park off the road near the trailhead. GPS Trailhead Coordinates: 34° 04' 25" N, -118° 54' 18" W

The Hike

This hike begins at the upper trailhead for Malibu Springs. Stay left and walk through the meadow, where outstanding views of the Santa Monica Mountains are simply par for the course. In less than 0.1 mile the trail branches into a Y, where the mountain views quickly subside. Turn left to follow the trail into Nicholas Flat—the right fork heads down to Malibu Springs.

At 0.25 mile the trail drops down along an old fence and a ranch road that returns to Decker School Road, passing through an old ranch gate. Go through the gate and follow the trail south, down the old road. This is the actual beginning of the trail, but the first quarter of a mile along the Malibu Springs Trail adds a significant amount of beauty to the route, and gives the hiker a taste of this section of the national recreation area.

Beyond the gate, the trail enters a sylvan woodland populated with oak and coastal chaparral. The trail follows the roadway for a little less than 0.5 mile and intersects with the actual signed trail on the right at a little over 0.6 mile. Do not turn: Stay on the old road and continue straight for another 0.1 mile, and then follow the old road as it turns left. On some maps this road is designated as Nicholas Ridge Motor Way.

The route opens up onto some rolling coastal hills. During winter through late spring, the hills should reflect a beautiful green, and wildflowers are common. Stay on the road and follow it out onto a promontory where views up and down the coastline are quite spectacular. Vistas of Anacapa, Santa Cruz, and Catalina Island are fairly common, with tiny Santa Barbara and San Nicholas being visible on

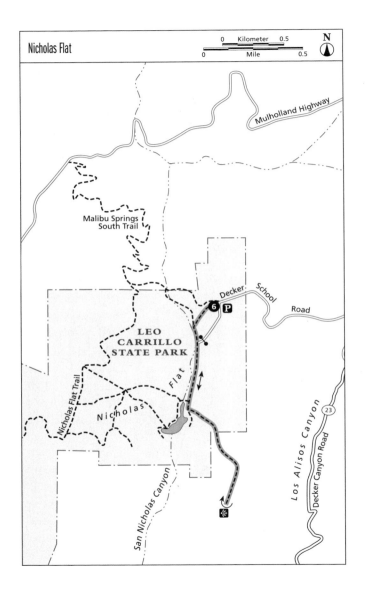

Nicholas Flat

Leo Carrillo State Park

Malibu Springs South Trail

Decker School Road

Nicholas Flat Trail

Nicholas Flat

San Nicholas Canyon

Los Alisos Canyon

Decker Canyon Road

Mulholland Highway

N

0   Kilometer   0.5
0   Mile   0.5

exceptionally clear days. The view of the coast is quite spectacular, and those unafraid of hiking back during twilight and possible darkness should stay to witness the sun dropping into the Pacific. It can be quite transcendental.

It is possible to follow the old road down to the Pacific Coast Highway, but return via the same route to the trailhead for Malibu Springs.

Miles and Directions

0.0 From the trailhead, walk west on the trail. Stay left at the Y intersection.

0.25 Go through the old gate and turn right onto Decker School Road. Walk down the old dirt road.

0.6 At the junction with the signed trail, stay straight and follow the old road as it turns left.

0.8 Turn right at the junction. Follow the road past a high point to a spot with outstanding coastal views.

1.3 Reach the turnaround point. Return via the same route.

2.6 Arrive back at the trailhead.

7 Charmlee Wilderness Park

Hike along a high coastal plain, overlooking magnificent vistas of Malibu and the clear blue of the Pacific.

Distance: 2.15-mile lollipop
Approximate hiking time: 1.5 hours
Elevation gain: 300 feet
Difficulty: Easy
Trail surface: Dirt and sand
Best season: Year-round; spring for wildflowers
Other trail users: None
Canine compatibility: Leashed dogs permitted
Fees and permits: A parking fee is charged.

Trail contact: Charmlee Wilderness Park, 2577 Encinal Canyon Rd., Malibu, CA 90265; (310) 457-7247; www.ci.malibu.ca .us/index.cfm/fuseaction/Detail Group/CID/3801/NavID/174/. Santa Monica Mountains National Recreation Area, 401 West Hillcrest Dr., Thousand Oaks, CA 91360; (805) 370-2301; www.nps.gov/samo/

Finding the trailhead: From the intersection of US 101 and Lindero Canyon Road in Westlake Village, take US 101 northwest for 1 mile. Take exit 40 for Westlake Boulevard/CA 23. Turn left onto South Westlake Boulevard/CA 23. Drive for 5.3 miles. CA 23 turns slightly right and becomes Mulholland Highway/CA 23. Drive for 0.2 miles. Turn slightly left to stay on Mulholland Highway/CA 23, and drive for 2.5 miles, following the signs for CA 23. (At 1.7 miles Mulholland Highway/CA 23 becomes Decker Canyon Road, continue on the CA 23 for 0.8 miles.) Turn left at Lechusa Road, drive for 0.1 mile, then continue straight as Lechusa Road becomes Encinal Canyon Road for 1.2 miles. Turn right onto Old Ranch Road/Carmichael Road at the entrance for Charmlee Wilderness Park. Drive for 0.3 miles to the parking area. GPS Trailhead Coordinates: 34° 03' 29" N, -118° 52' 45" W

The Hike

Charmlee Wilderness Park is managed and owned by the city of Malibu, but is incorporated into the larger Santa Monica Mountains National Recreation Area. While admittance is free, parking is not. No doubt there will be some people that choose to park along Encinal Canyon Road, avoiding the parking fee while adding 0.5 mile to the overall trip. However, don't be a cheapskate. This is an astonishingly beautiful area with a splendid nature center and clean restrooms. Think of it as a worthwhile cause. Natural areas are horribly underfunded in the state of California. Charmlee Wilderness Park could easily be renamed Charming Wilderness Park, as most visitors will be truly won over on their first visit.

A free brochure is available at the entrance park kiosk. The map provided on the brochure is really a rough guide, not very well oriented, marked, or scaled. It may just lend more to confusion than navigation, but those with a good sense of direction, and who are eager for some pirate treasure map-style adventure, may want to chart out a course and try to follow it. Everyone else should simply forget about seeing all of the highlights and simply stroll along the wide old ranch road, which is the route described and mapped here. There are many cutoff trails and side branches from the main route that can be explored. Visitors can pick and choose whichever they desire. However, do be aware that narrow paths meandering through tall grasses often conceal ticks and surreptitiously hidden poison oak. Those with children would do well to stay on wider tracks and on the main trail that rambles through the park.

So many side trails intersect with the main trail(s) that it is difficult to keep track of them all, but for those looking to duplicate the route marked on the map, it is rather simple. From the parking lot and restrooms, walk straight and south along Old Ranch Road/Carmichael Road, heading toward the coast. Avoid the first two trails on the left and right, and continue straight along the widest road which leads to the Meadow Ranch Trail. Turn left at 0.3 mile. Avoid the next two junctions and turn right at 0.4 mile, heading south across the flat meadow along the Meadow Ranch Trail toward the old reservoir and the coastal view.

At 0.8 mile turn left and climb up to the reservoir. Views stretch down to the ocean, and the scenery is splendidly magnificent. Continue past the reservoir on the wide trail, avoiding all of the smaller junctions. Stay on the wide path as it hairpins, and turn left at the 1.1-mile mark. The trail meanders through some oak woodland and joins up with an even wider trail at 1.3 miles. Continue straight and to the right here, on the largest path. Follow this to a junction at 1.6 miles and turn left, crossing the meadow. At 1.7 miles the trail rejoins the original road back to the parking area.

Those wishing to visit the nature center should turn left at the restrooms and walk a short distance up the road.

Miles and Directions

0.0 From the restrooms, walk south along Old Ranch Road/Carmichael Road.

0.3 Turn left at the first main junction.

0.4 Turn right at the next main junction and head south along the Meadow Ranch Trail toward the old reservoir and the obvious coastal viewpoint.

0.8 Turn left and climb up to the old reservoir.

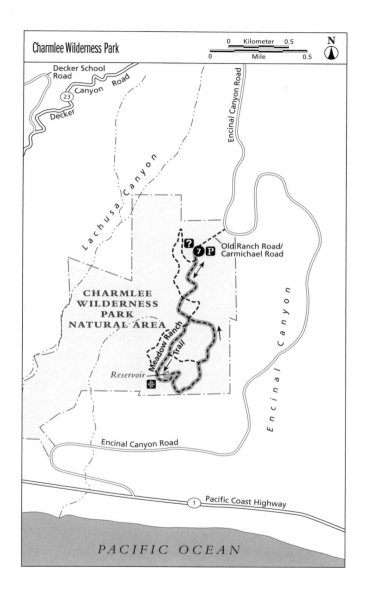

Charmlee Wilderness Park

0 Kilometer 0.5
0 Mile 0.5

N

Decker School
Road

Canyon Road

23

Decker

Encinal Canyon Road

Lachusa Canyon

? 7 P

Old Ranch Road/
Carmichael Road

CHARMLEE
WILDERNESS
PARK
NATURAL AREA

Meadow Ranch Trail

Reservoir

Encinal Canyon

Encinal Canyon Road

1 Pacific Coast Highway

PACIFIC OCEAN

1.1 Turn left after the hairpin turn in the wide trail.

1.3 Continue straight and to the right, on the widest path, after walking through the oak woodland.

1.6 Turn left at the junction and walk across the meadow.

1.7 Rejoin Old Ranch Road/Carmichael Road and continue straight.

1.8 Turn right at the junction, closing the loop and retracing your steps.

2.15 Arrive back at the trailhead, restrooms, and parking area.

8 Paradise Falls (Wildwood Park)

Hike through a lovely suburban park to a towering and dazzling 50-foot waterfall.

Distance: 2.3-mile loop
Approximate hiking time: 1.5 hours
Elevation gain: 550 feet
Difficulty: Easy
Trail surface: Dirt and sand
Best season: Year-round; spring and shortly after rains for the highest water volume. The park may close periodically after heavy rains due to high and dangerous volumes of water.
Other trail users: Bicyclists, equestrians
Canine compatibility: Leashed dogs permitted
Fees and permits: None
Trail contact: Conejo Open Space Conservation Agency (COSCA), 2100 Thousand Oaks Blvd., Thousand Oaks, CA 91362; (805) 381-2741 or (805) 402-9551. Conejo Open Space Foundation, P.O. Box 2113, Thousand Oaks, CA 91358; www.cosf.org

Finding the trailhead: From the intersection of US 101 and Lindero Canyon Road in Westlake Village, take US 101 northwest for 5.5 miles. Take exit 45 for Lynn Road. Turn right onto Lynn Road and drive for 2.5 miles. Turn left onto Avenida de los Arboles. Drive for 0.9 mile and park in the lot on the left. GPS Trailhead Coordinates: 34° 13' 12" N, -118° 54' 08" W

The Hike

Wildwood Canyon is an exercise mecca for those in the Conejo Valley. It is a favorite of hikers, mountain bikers, schoolchildren, and anyone looking for a little bit of outdoor adventure with a spectacular payoff. It is extensively marked and signed. There are many different trails and routes and lots of interesting things to see in Wildwood Canyon, but nothing as outstanding as the 50-foot waterfall that pours over limestone into a large pool lined by oaks, sycamore, and cattails. There isn't as remarkable a waterfall anywhere else in the Conejo Valley, and there are only a few that cascade so vigorously and beautifully in all of Southern California. Paradise Falls is a treasure unknown to most outside of the region, but is heavily visited by those in the know.

While many people use the park as an oversized exercise facility, there are ways to walk along the routes less traveled. For one, stay off the broad main roads and take the less-visited trail. After all, this is a hike and not a drive. From the parking lot, most people walk west, up the hill past the informational kiosk onto the Mesa Trail, heading to the falls via a variety of widely spaced, well signed, open, and crowded (but closed to vehicle traffic) roadways. Instead of following the crowd, head east and walk down the stairs leading to the Moonridge Trail.

Not as wild as the park's name would suggest, houses and wires are visible along the entire route. Taking the Moonridge Trail will certainly eliminate contact with 98 to 99 percent of the people walking through the park. The trail follows the canyon wall of a smaller fork of the North Fork Arroyo Conejo drainage. The trail wanders through brambly chaparral and can be hot and dusty even during wetter and colder periods of the year, depending upon the weather.

While the trail is not spectacularly beautiful, the end in this case truly justifies the means. At 0.45 mile the Moonridge Trail intersects an old access road: Continue straight across the road and stay on the Moonridge Trail toward

Paradise Falls. The route continues to wind alongside the canyon until it intersects a road called North Tepee Trail at 0.9 mile. Turn left and walk toward the large inauthentic tepee where children and families gather for shade, repast, and respite. The tepee is 1 mile from the start of the hike.

Turn right along Tepee Trail and follow the signs for Paradise Falls. From this point Arroyo Conejo can be seen, and if the water is flowing it can also be heard. Lush riparian woodland lines the creekbed and the trail steeply descends toward the bottom. At 1.15 miles turn left onto the smaller Paradise Falls Trail. Follow it to a picnic area and smaller branch that leads to the spectacular waterfall at 1.25 miles.

Despite a fence and some visible improvements above the falls, the view is truly stunning. There is a good-size pool for swimming, but signs recommend against it due to the creek being fed by both natural means and by street and storm drain runoff. Enjoy the views, relax, and reflect upon the awesome natural beauty that is quite unexpected in this canyon.

Return to the tepee at 1.5 miles, and turn left up North Tepee Trail. Hike to the end of the road and turn right on the Mesa Trail at 1.9 miles. Follow the Mesa Trail back to the parking area.

Miles and Directions

0.0 From the parking area, head east and descend the steps to the Moonridge Trail.

0.45 Cross the old access road and continue west along the Moonridge Trail.

0.9 Turn left onto North Tepee Trail.

1.0 Arrive at the tepee structure and turn right onto Tepee Trail.

1.15 Turn left onto Paradise Falls Trail.

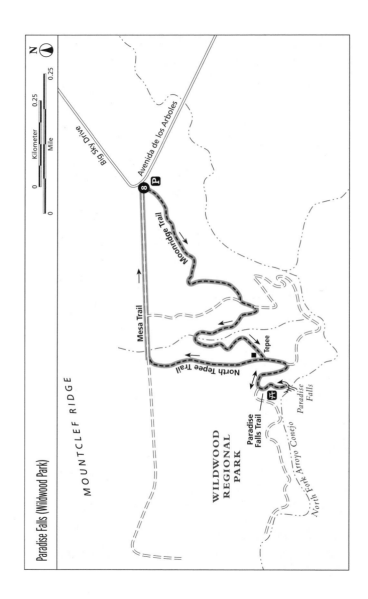

Paradise Falls (Wildwood Park)

MOUNTCLEF RIDGE

Big Sky Drive

Avenida de los Arboles

N

Kilometer
0   0.25

Mile
0   0.25

Mesa Trail

Moonridge Trail

North Tepee Trail

Tepee

Paradise Falls Trail

Paradise Falls

WILDWOOD REGIONAL PARK

North Fork Arroyo Conejo

1.25 Arrive at Paradise Falls. Return to the tepee via the same route.

1.5 Arrive at the tepee and turn left onto North Tepee Trail.

1.9 Turn right onto Mesa Trail and return to the parking area.

2.3 Arrive at the trailhead and parking area.

⃝9 Sunset Hills

Hike to a lovely ridgeline with spectacular city and lake views.

Distance: 2.4 miles out and back
Approximate hiking time: 1.5 hours
Elevation gain: 500 feet
Difficulty: Easy
Trail surface: Dirt
Best season: Year-round; hot in summer
Other trail users: Equestrians, bicyclists

Canine compatibility: Leashed dogs permitted
Fees and permits: None
Trail contact: Conejo Open Space Conservation Agency (COSCA), 2100 Thousand Oaks Blvd., Thousand Oaks, CA 91362; (805) 381-2741 or (805) 402-9551. Conejo Open Space Foundation, P.O. Box 2113, Thousand Oaks, CA 91358; www.cosf.org

Finding the trailhead: From the intersection of US 101 and Lindero Canyon Road in Westlake Village, take US 101 northwest for 3.2 miles. Exit onto CA 23 north and drive for 4 miles. Take the Sunset Hills Boulevard exit. Turn right onto Sunset Hills Boulevard. Drive for 0.2 mile. Take the first left onto Erbes Road. Drive for 0.7 mile. Turn right into the parking area. GPS Trailhead Coordinates: 34° 13' 57" N, -118° 50' 19" W

The Hike

Although this is not quite the hike for those looking to get away from it all—CA 23 is close by and suburban sprawl is ubiquitous—it is a wonderful place to get some quick exercise and take in some views.

For the amount of elevation gain on this hike, the views are more than rewarding. They could even be called spectacular, except for the chain-link fence that borders the boundary of the Wood Ranch Reservoir. Despite the fence, however, the surrounding mountains, the reservoir, and the open countryside are all quite breathtaking. The hike leads to a high prominence along a ridgeline in the Simi Hills, and at nearly 1,600 feet, it is the highest point around, affording 360-degree views. The Wood Ranch Reservoir sits below the trail and ridgeline to the north, creating a wonderful focal point for those hiking along the spine of the hill. While there is considerable open space to the east, the south is filled with large homes, some of which climb the hillside close to the trail.

From the pullout parking area on Erbes Road, walk along the trail at the north end of the parking lot. The trail steadily climbs up the side of the hill, and within 0.5 mile, Wood Ranch Reservoir can be spotted.

After gaining the ridgeline, the reservoir is prominent to the north for the rest of the hike and the trail follows the fence line. The trail continues to climb gently and steadily, passing some homes just below the ridge on the south at 1 mile. Continue straight and hike to the obvious high point 0.25 mile beyond to the east. At this spot, the views are quite lovely. It is a good place to take a rest before beginning the journey back to the parking area. Retrace your steps to the trailhead.

This trail is a great training hike. The relatively short distance makes it excellent for those with only an hour or so to hike in the evenings. It is a great place to run and train for moderate elevation gains. Hiking a trail like this four

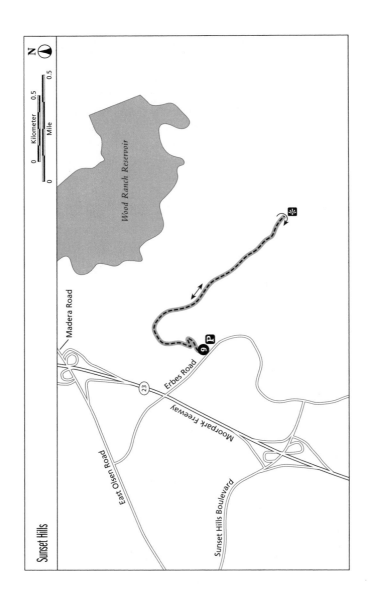

Sunset Hills

to six times a week will prepare anyone for longer treks of greater distances.

Miles and Directions

0.0 From the parking area, take the trail at the back of the lot.

0.25 Ignore the two spur trails on the left. Continue straight.

0.35 Turn right at the fork.

0.5 Follow the fence for the remainder of the hike.

1.2 Reach the high point. Return via the same route.

2.4 Arrive back at the trailhead and parking area.

10 Los Robles Trail

Take a walk along the open ridgeline on the Conejo Open Space Conservation Agency's longest trail. This section of the Los Robles Trail starts along the Rosewood Trail in Ventu Park and passes through the Hope Nature Preserve and Los Robles Open Space Preserve.

Distance: 3.5 miles point to point
Approximate hiking time: 2 hours
Elevation gain: 700 feet
Difficulty: Easy
Trail surface: Dirt
Best season: Fall through spring; hot in summer; may be closed during rains and fire season
Other trail users: None

Canine compatibility: Leashed dogs permitted
Fees and permits: None
Trail contact: Conejo Open Space Conservation Agency (COSCA), 2100 Thousand Oaks Blvd., Thousand Oaks, CA 91362; (805) 381-2741 or (805) 402-9551. Conejo Open Space Foundation, P.O. Box 2113, Thousand Oaks, CA 91358; www.cosf.org

Finding the trailhead: From the intersection of US 101 and Lindero Canyon Road in Westlake Village, take US 101 northwest for 6.5 miles. Take exit 46 for Ventu Park Road towards Newbury Park. Turn left onto North Ventu Park Road and drive for 0.6 mile. Turn right onto Lynn Road, drive for 0.3 mile. Turn left onto Regal Oak Court, drive to the end, obey parking signs and park a shuttle car. The trail runs through the open space on the east (34° 10' 21" N, -118° 54' 50" W). Once the shuttle car is parked, head north on Regal Oak Court for 0.3 mile. Turn right onto Lynn Road. Drive for 1.5 miles. Take the on ramp for US 101 South. Drive for 0.8 mile. Take Exit 44 for Moorpark Road. Turn right onto South Moorpark Road.

Drive for 0.5 mile to the end of the road and park in the large Los Robles Trail parking lot. A sign marks the start of the trail. GPS Trailhead Coordinates: 34° 10' 19" N, -118° 52' 52" W

The Hike

The Los Robles Trail is a part of the Conejo Open Space and connects several open space areas in the Conejo Valley, including Los Padres, Conejo Ridge, Hope Nature Preserve, Deer Ridge, Old Conejo, and Los Vientos. Twenty-five miles of trail connect the city of Westlake Village to Newbury Park. This trail traverses a beautiful 3.5-mile ridgeline section from the Los Robles Open Space through the Hope Nature Preserve. The views are spectacular, and the trail demonstrates just what open space parks should be across the nation.

From the parking area at the end of South Moorpark Road, walk west into the open space. Ignore the smaller route on the left that leads uphill, staying on the wider path. At 0.25 mile, where the trail triangles, stay to the right. Just beyond the triangle, at 0.35 miles, turn left onto the Los Robles Trail.

This trail is surrounded by coastal chaparral and shrubby plants. It is a fairly obvious route because it is the one that appears to lead uphill—and it does. The trail begins by following a canyon but quickly climbs by switchbacking up a ridge. The trail gains incredible views, and stays just under the ridge for most of the route. Along the way it tops out at awesome views of the Conejo Valley.

At 2.2 miles the trail crosses dirt Ventu Park Road, continue straight on the trail. After the road, a confluence of trails can lead to some confusion. Turn right at the first junction at 2.4 miles. At the next four-way junction, take

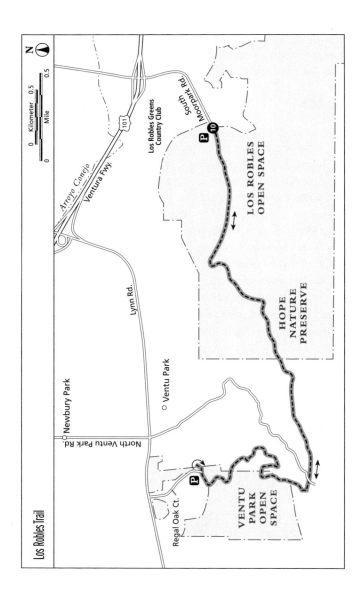

Los Robles Trail

the middle fork and continue straight. This will lead to the parking area along Regal Oak Court.

Those who want to do this hike as an out-and-back can turn around and return as they came. Those who parked a shuttle car can drive back to the trailhead.

Miles and Directions

0.0 From the parking lot at the end of South Moorpark Road, walk west into the preserve. Within the first 0.1 mile, take the trail on the left.

0.25 At the trail triangle, stay right.

0.35 Turn left onto the Los Robles Trail and head up the canyon to the ridgeline.

2.2 Cross Ventu Park Road; stay straight on the trail.

2.4 Turn right at the trail junction. At the next four-way junction, stay straight, taking the middle fork.

3.5 Arrive at the parking area on Regal Oak Court. Return as you came, or shuttle back to South Moorpark Road.

11 Lake Eleanor Open Space

Hike along a lovely ridge and enjoy fantastic views of Lake Eleanor, Lake Sherwood, and Las Virgenes Reservoir.

Distance: 2.6 miles out and back
Approximate hiking time: 1.5 hours
Elevation gain: 500 feet
Difficulty: Easy
Trail surface: Dirt
Best season: Year-round; hot in summer
Other trail users: Trail runners
Canine compatibility: Leashed

dogs allowed
Fees and permits: None
Trail contact: Conejo Open Space Conservation Agency (COSCA), 2100 Thousand Oaks Blvd., Thousand Oaks, CA 91362; (805) 381-2741 or (805) 402-9551. Conejo Open Space Foundation, P.O. Box 2113, Thousand Oaks, CA 91358; www.cosf.org

Finding the trailhead: From the intersection of US 101 and Lindero Canyon Road, head south on Lindero Canyon Road for 1.8 miles. Turn right onto Triunfo Canyon Road. Drive for 0.9 mile. Turn left onto Three Springs Drive and drive for 0.8 mile. Turn right onto Kristen Lee Drive and drive for 0.8 mile. Turn right onto Denver Springs Drive and drive for 0.2 mile. Park along the roadside and do not block driveways. GPS Trailhead Coordinates: 34° 07' 44" N, -118° 51' 09" W

The Hike

This trail starts off in one neighborhood, and ends in a different neighborhood. While most would assume this kind of hike would not include amazing scenery, that would be a horrible assumption. The mountain and lake views on this trip are truly incredible. Pointed peaks dart above the horizon, while sparkling liquid jewels glimmer in blue below. Yes, tracts of houses do enter the views along the trail, but there are many places along the route where it is possible to forget just how close to suburban civilization this trail really is. The terrain is rugged and quite rocky, and in some spots it is easy to lose footing, but it is a worthwhile trip for anyone. It is relatively free of strenuous elevation gains—surprisingly flat given that the trail follows the ridgeline for the entire distance.

From the cul-de-sac parking area, follow the trail north along the ridgeline. The trail climbs sharply at first, gaining views rather quickly into the hike. And what views they are! Lake Eleanor, to the west, seems within diving distance, and Lake Sherwood, Westlake, and the Las Virgenes Reservoir make this area look more like an alpine canyon than an arid Southern California coastal landscape. The houses only detract slightly, and it is interesting to note how the builders made use of the natural landscape to craft homes out of the canyon bottom.

Hike along the ridge for 1.3 miles. There are a variety of small use trails that lead to various highpoints along the way. Those with lots of energy may wish to explore every one. At the end of the trail, the route descends to Hillsbury Road. This is the turnaround, as this trek is an out-and-back hike. The views on the way out are just as amazing as on the way in.

The only bad thing about this trail is that the open space is so small. At the end of the route on Hillsbury Road there just isn't anywhere else left to explore. Hikers will not feel disappointed, though, and people wishing to use this as an exercise route won't be let down either.

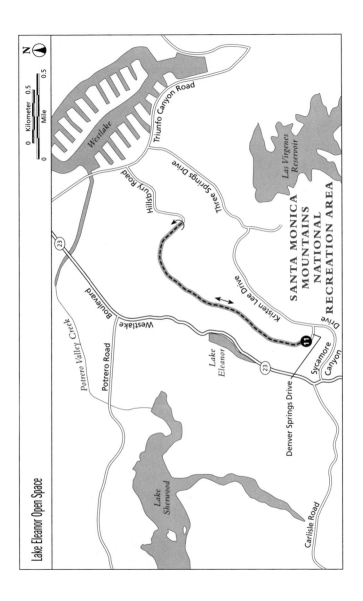

Lake Eleanor Open Space

SANTA MONICA
MOUNTAINS NATIONAL
RECREATION AREA

Westlake

Las Virgenes
Reservoir

Triunfo Canyon Road

Three Springs Drive

Hillsbury Road

Kristen Lee Drive

Sycamore
Canyon
Drive

Westlake Boulevard

Potrero Valley Creek

Potrero Road

Lake
Eleanor

Denver Springs Drive

Lake
Sherwood

Carlisle Road

N

0   Kilometer   0.5
0   Mile   0.5

Miles and Directions

0.0 Walk north from the cul-de-sac parking area at the end of Denver Springs Drive.

1.0 Turn right at the fork.

1.3 Turn around at Hillsbury Road. Return via the same route.

2.6 Arrive back at the trailhead parking area.

12 Paramount Ranch

Hike through a movie/television set and along a quaint hillside to an overlook of Western Town set and region.

Distance: 1.6-mile double loop
Approximate hiking time: 1 hour
Elevation gain: 200 feet
Difficulty: Easy
Trail surface: Dirt
Best season: Fall through spring; hot in summer
Other trail users: Trail runners
Canine compatibility: Leashed dogs permitted

Fees and permits: None
Trail contact: Paramount Ranch, 2903 Cornell Rd., Agoura Hills, CA 91301; www.nps.gov/samo/planyourvisit/paramountranch .htm. Santa Monica Mountains National Recreation Area, 401 West Hillcrest Dr., Thousand Oaks, CA 91360; (805) 370-2301; www.nps.gov/samo

Finding the trailhead: From the intersection of US 101 and Lindero Canyon Road in Westlake Village, head southeast on US 101 for 2.3 miles. Take exit 36 for Kanan Road. Turn right onto Kanan Road and drive 0.4 mile. Turn left at Sideway/Cornell Road. Drive for 1.9 miles. Turn right into Paramount Ranch and continue to the visitor center. GPS Trailhead Coordinates: 34° 06' 57" N, -118° 45' 17" W

The Hike

Paramount Ranch is a pretty cool place. In 1927 Paramount Pictures bought the land and used it as a set for many major motion pictures of the day. Fans of old black-and-white movies will undoubtedly feel a familiarity from the outset. Films featuring Buster Crabbe, Mae West, Marlene

Dietrich, Gary Cooper, Leo Carillo, Randolph Scott, and many others were shot here before Paramount eventually sold the land in the 1950s. A man named William Hertz bought a portion and turned part of the parcel, still named Paramount Ranch, into a model of an old western town. Filming resumed almost immediately, mostly of westerns and television shows such as *The Cisco Kid*. The land was eventually purchased by the National Park Service in 1980, and filming still occurs there to this day, although less frequently.

As a visitor, you get to walk around the western town that has served as a television and movie backdrop. Most visitors to the park will be familiar with its most recent shot at fame: *Dr. Quinn Medicine Woman* filmed at the park exclusively from 1992 to 1997. As a national park site, the ranch is free to enter and explore. It is unique in that it is the only national park site where you can see movie-making in action.

From the entrance and parking area, free brochures are available that display the trails and routes through and around the park. There are also several interactive signs near the entrance to the park. Walk south along the roadway toward the old western set and cross the footbridge at 0.1 mile into the town. From a distance, the set looks real enough to be an old ghost town, and it is only upon further inspection that it becomes obvious it's a facade. Although the western town is small, there is enough to look at to keep even smaller children in awe for a while.

Walking west along the roadway through the town will lead past the replica train depot at 0.2 mile to the Coyote Canyon Trail. Follow this short loop along a nice little intermittent creek. At a point 0.4 mile into the hike, turn

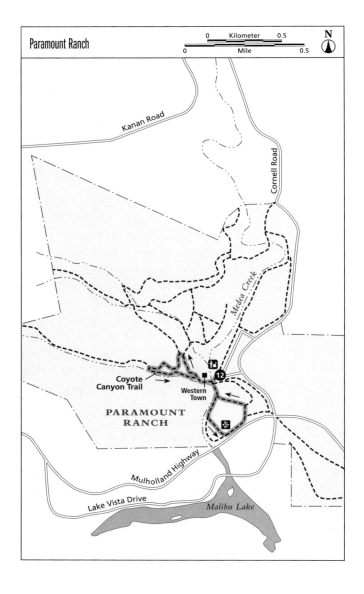

Paramount Ranch

Kanan Road

Cornell Road

Medea Creek

Coyote
Canyon Trail

Western
Town

PARAMOUNT
RANCH

Mulholland Highway

Lake Vista Drive

Malibu Lake

N

0   Kilometer   0.5
0   Mile   0.5

right at the junction to stay on the loop. The trail enters into a more open area, and eventually reaches another junction at 0.7 mile. Turn right again and head back to the western town.

Walk across the footbridge and turn right onto the road. Follow the dirt road as it parallels Medea Creek. The Medea Creek Trail strolls through an oak forest along the creekside and branches left, heading southeast toward Mulholland Highway at 1 mile. At the next junction, turn left to the hilltop lookout. This is a particularly satisfying overlook for anyone who has ever played cowboys and Indians. Go back to the branch and turn left again. Turn left at the next junction and walk back toward the parking area.

Miles and Directions

0.0 From the parking area head south along the road.

0.1 Turn right and cross the footbridge into the western town.

0.2 Pass the replica rail station and enter the Coyote Canyon Trail.

0.4 Turn right at the junction to stay on the Coyote Canyon loop.

0.7 Turn right and head back to the western town.

0.8 Cross the footbridge and turn right onto the road.

1.0 Follow the trail left to the short spur to the overlook.

1.25 Arrive at the overlook spur, turn left. Return to the trail.

1.35 Turn left and return to the road.

1.5 Turn right and return to the parking area.

1.6 Arrive back at the trailhead and parking lot.

13 Malibu Creek

Hike through lovely Malibu Creek State Park, walking along the creek to the television set for *M*A*S*H*.

Distance: 5 miles out and back

Approximate hiking time: 2.5 hours

Elevation gain: 550 feet

Difficulty: Moderate

Trail surface: Dirt

Best season: Year-round; hot in summer

Other trail users: Mountain bikers, equestrians, trail runners

Canine compatibility: Dogs not permitted

Fees and permits: A day use fee is charged.

Trail contact: Malibu Creek State Park, 1925 Las Virgenes Rd., Calabasas, CA 91302; (818) 880-0367; www.parks.ca.gov/ default.asp?page_id=614. Santa Monica Mountains National Recreation Area, 401 West Hillcrest Dr., Thousand Oaks, CA 91360; (805) 370-2301; www.nps.gov/ samo

Finding the trailhead: From the intersection of US 101 and Lindero Canyon Road in Westlake Village, head southeast on US 101 for 5.3 miles. Take exit 33 for Lost Hills Road. Turn right onto Lost Hills Road and drive 1.1 miles. Turn right at Las Virgenes Road. Drive for 1.8 miles. Turn right into Malibu Creek State Park, and continue 0.4 mile to the trailhead parking area. GPS Trailhead Coordinates: 34° 05' 46" N, -118° 43' 01" W

The Hike

Malibu Creek State Park is a popular destination for many types of recreationalists. Campers, hikers, rock climbers, horseback riders, bicyclists, and families all love this park—and with good reason, as it is quite beautiful and has a lot to offer. Countless films and TV shows have made the park's natural features famous. The landscape doubled for Korea in the TV show *M★A★S★H,* a future Earth in *Planet of the Apes,* Mexico for Marlon Brando in *Viva Zapata!,* and more. There are simply too many to mention. If hikers have a good eye and keep a diligent lookout, film locations are quite easy to spot. Beside the nostalgia though, the park is simply breathtaking. To not include it in a best easy day hikes book would be almost criminal.

To say that a lot of people use this park is an understatement. Often the parking lot is near capacity and the trails are always teeming with people. However, it does not make the hike seem overcrowded, just busy. Of course the farther you go into the park means less people, as the majority stay near the visitor center, Century Lake, and a swimming hole just off of the Crags Fire Road Trail. Not as many people make the trek to the *M★A★S★H* site, and as that show fades deeper into history, perhaps even less will. But it is a terrific journey nonetheless.

From the parking area, walk along the main road west into the park, follow the High Road Trail (this is the widest trail in the park and it is still an accessible road for the Park Service) as it skirts alongside Malibu Creek through incredibly large old oaks. These beautiful trees make a magnificent canopy to stroll and picnic under. At 0.9 mile turn left and cross the footbridge to the visitor center, an old adobe dwelling called Century Ranch. Small children are certain to love the displays and older folks just might learn a thing or two as well.

Return to the main trail and hike up the old road around a bend. Descend right next to Century Lake, an idyllic spot for shooting photos. Continue west along the trail. At

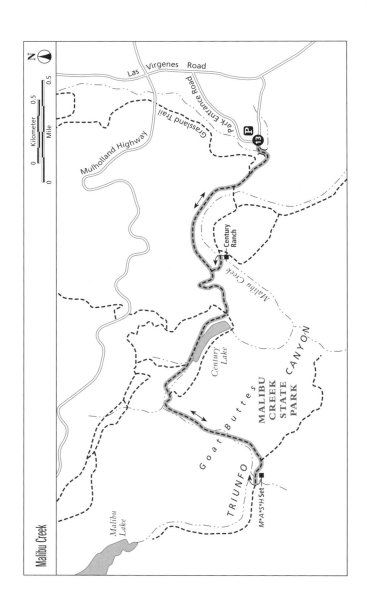

right around 2 miles the trail narrows from lack of usage, although in part it remains an old road. It follows a side branch of Triunfo Canyon between the aptly named Goat Buttes. These protruding rocks formed the backdrop for many a television episode, and their craggy looks make for interesting conjecture.

After entering a clearing, what is left of the old M*A*S*H film site comes into view. A ruined jeep and a rusty ambulance are all that is left. The scenery is unmistakable. Return via the same route.

Miles and Directions

0.0 From the parking area head west along the High Road Trail.

0.2 Keep straight at the junction with the Grassland Trail.

0.4 Stay right at the fork.

0.9 Turn left and cross the footbridge toward the visitor center/ Century Ranch.

1.0 Arrive at visitor center/Century Ranch. Cross back over the footbridge.

1.1 Return to High Road and head west up the hillside.

1.4 Arrive at Century Lake.

1.75 Stay straight at the junction with the Reagan Ranch Trail.

2.0 Follow the trail through a branch of Triunfo Canyon.

2.6 Arrive at the M*A*S*H site. Return via the same route.

5.0 Arrive back at the trailhead and parking area.

14 China Flat Trail

Walk to a high plateau in the picturesque Simi Hills.

Distance: 5.75-mile lollipop
Approximate hiking time: 3 hours
Elevation gain: 1,400 feet
Difficulty: Moderate
Trail surface: Dirt
Best season: Fall through spring; hot in summer
Other trail users: Mountain bikers, trail runners, equestrians
Canine compatibility: Leashed dogs permitted

Fees and permits: None
Trail contact: Cheeseboro/Palo Comado Canyons, 5792 Chesebro Rd., Agoura, CA 91301; www.nps.gov/samo/planyour visit/cheeseboropalocomado .htm. Santa Monica Mountains National Recreation Area, 401 West Hillcrest Dr., Thousand Oaks, CA 91360; (805) 370-2301; www.nps.gov/samo

Finding the trailhead: From the intersection of US 101 and Lindero Canyon Road in Westlake Village, head north on Lindero Canyon Road for 3.9 miles. Park on the north side of the road. The trail begins in an unsigned open space between two housing subdivisions. GPS Trailhead Coordinates: 34° 11' 37" N, -118° 46' 30" W

The Hike

The Simi Hills are often overlooked as dry and dusty. Typically cast as hot and suburban, with too much humanity and not enough nature, the hills are really only frequented by those who live nearby. While on hot days the best bet is to climb early in the morning or as the evening is settling into dusk, during the cooler times of the year, the hills are quite beautiful at any time of day. In spring, lovely wildflowers bloom alongside the trail. The rocks are uniquely interesting to those with geologic interests, in that they are very old and display significant strata caused by tectonic shifts. For the layperson the rock formations just look incredibly cool. Most people fail to notice the colors and layers from the highway, but up close the tints and features are even more punctuated.

This trail travels up the China Flat Trail (an old road) to Simi Peak, and then through China Flat itself before making a loop and returning to the trailhead. From street parking along Lindero Canyon Road, head north into the national park unit. The trail wanders between housing tracts and reaches an old dirt road. Follow this to the north as it winds and switchbacks up the hillside. The main route is fairly easy to follow and most side routes double back up with the main trail. Follow the widest roadway up and routefinding is quite simple.

At 0.8 mile the trail hairpins and heads eastward. The first mile of the hike is quite steep and a good workout. Gaining 1,000 feet of elevation in 1 mile is pretty much the standard for climbing really tall mountains, so those looking to use this as an exercise route or a training hike for larger peaks would be well advised to do so.

At 1.25 miles, follow the left fork leading into China Flat. Continue straight into the oak-lined flat. The views are quite nice from the plateau. The flat is an awesome meadow complete with a vernal pool in wet times. The area seems to be a relic of California's rustic past. Walking through the region feels like stepping into history.

The views get better on top of Simi Peak. At 1.6 miles, turn left and follow the main road through the flat toward

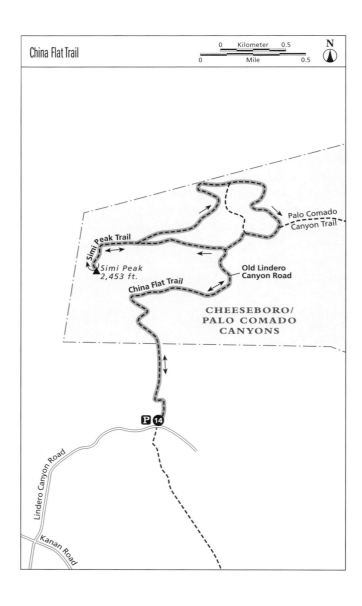

China Flat Trail

0   Kilometer   0.5
0   Mile   0.5

N

Simi Peak Trail

Simi Peak
2,453 ft.

China Flat Trail

Palo Comado
Canyon Trail

Old Lindero
Canyon Road

CHEESEBORO/
PALO COMADO
CANYONS

P 14

Lindero Canyon Road

Kanan Road

the peak to the west. Once atop Simi Peak, a 360-degree view greets hikers. To the south, the Conejo Valley is spread across the horizon, and the canyons of Simi Valley can be viewed in all their greatness. There is quite a bit of open space, so the area seems fairly wild given its proximity to civilization.

After leaving the summit, take the left intersection at 2.6 miles. This route makes a lollipop through China Flat: Hikers can wander alongside the edge of Lone Oak Canyon before returning to the main route. From here, retrace your steps back to the street-side parking.

Miles and Directions

0.0 From Lindero Canyon Road, head north into the national park. Follow the main route.

0.8 Turn eastward at the hairpin.

1.25 Follow the left fork into China Flat. Stay on the main trail.

1.6 Turn left and head west toward Simi Peak along the old road.

2.25 Arrive atop Simi Peak. Turn around and descend via the same route.

2.6 Take the left intersecting trail (34° 12' 24" N, -118° 46' 39" W).

3.4 Stay straight on the trail at the intersection with old Lindero Canyon Road.

3.9 Turn right onto old Palo Comado Fire Road/Trail.

4.1 Turn left onto old Lindero Canyon Road.

4.25 Return to the main route. Follow the trail back toward the parking area.

5.75 Arrive back at the trailhead parking.

15 Cheeseboro/Palo Comado Canyon Loop

Walk through two beautifully wooded canyons and along a ridgeline on this peaceful loop hike.

Distance: 6.6-mile loop

Approximate hiking time: 3.5 hours

Elevation gain: 800 feet

Difficulty: Moderate

Trail surface: Dirt

Best season: Late fall through early spring; spring for wildflowers; fall for autumn colors; hot in summer

Other trail users: Trail runners, bicyclists, equestrians

Canine compatibility: Leashed dogs permitted

Fees and permits: None

Trail contact: Cheeseboro/Palo Comado Canyons, 5792 Chesebro Rd., Agoura, CA 91301; www.nps.gov/samo/planyour visit/cheeseboropalocomado .htm. Santa Monica Mountains National Recreation Area, 401 West Hillcrest Dr., Thousand Oaks, CA 91360; (805) 370-2301; www.nps.gov/samo

Finding the trailhead: From the intersection of US 101 and Lindero Canyon Road in Westlake Village, head southeast on US 101 for 3.5 miles. Take exit 35 for Chesebro Road. Make a slight right onto Chesebro Road and drive for 0.1 mile. Turn left onto Palo Comado Canyon Road and drive for 0.3 mile. Turn right onto Chesebro Road and drive for 0.7 mile. Turn right onto Cheseboro Canyon Road and drive for 0.2 mile to the obvious and signed parking area. GPS Trailhead Coordinates: 34° 09' 23" N, -118° 43' 50" W

The Hike

The Simi Hills are an often overlooked area for hiking, due to the heat of summer and suburban environs. However, Cheeseboro Canyon is a lovely slice of shaded oak woodland great for exploring throughout the year. Granted, evenings and early mornings are a much better time to go for a hike in summer than midday, but the region has a pastoral charm making it a wonderful place for an outing at any time. A favorite of bicyclists, as the trail is shaded and easily accessible from the road, there will almost surely be mountain bikers sharing the trail.

The park is quiet and bucolic, old ranch roads dominate, and the scenery is both peaceful and idyllic. While there aren't spectacular falls or lofty peak views, the trail is truly a nice place to stroll. A picnic area offers visitors a chance to enjoy the quiet of the great outdoors. In spring, wildflowers dominate with lovely hues of yellow, orange, and purple. In the fall—early October through November—expect to see reds, oranges, and yellows. In Southern California, one has to know where to look to find the signs of fall; riparian canyons are definitely the best spots.

From the parking area, follow the Cheeseboro Canyon Trail east and north. There are lots of intersecting routes and paths, but hikers will want to stay within the confines of the shaded canyon. At times the trail merges with the old fire road, and the road simply becomes the trail. It isn't difficult to stay on the main route as the canyon bottom is quite obvious and the trail skirts alongside it.

At 2.4 miles, the Ranch Center connector trail intersects on the left. Take the Ranch Center Trail and begin the climb up to the hills that separate Palo Comado Canyon from Cheeseboro Canyon. At the top, nice views of the parkland and the Conejo Valley open up, and the trail gains its highest point at 2.9 miles.

From the high point the Ranch Center Trail descends back into shade and Palo Comado Canyon. Turn left onto the Palo Comado Canyon Trail at 3.4 miles, and begin walking south. The trail once again skirts alongside a canyon bottom dotted with lovely oak and riparian woodland.

Follow Palo Comado Canyon back to Chesebro Road, which intersects the trail at 4.5 miles. Turn left to stay on the Palo Comado Connector Trail. The trail again leaves the canyon bottom, making a short climb to the connector with the Modelo Trail. At 5.4 miles turn left and follow the Modelo Trail back to the trailhead and parking lot.

Miles and Directions

0.0 From the parking area head west along the Cheeseboro Canyon Trail.

0.25 Turn left at the first fork. Stay on the main route, which is Cheeseboro Canyon Trail.

0.6 Stay to the right on Cheeseboro Canyon Trail.

0.75 Stay to the left at the fork, following the path through the canyon.

1.3 Turn left at the fork. Stay to the right and straight at the next junction, and continue past the picnic area.

1.55 Ignore the fork to the right; continue straight.

1.9 Stay straight at the fork, though both paths converge farther on.

2.4 Turn left at the Ranch Center connector trail.

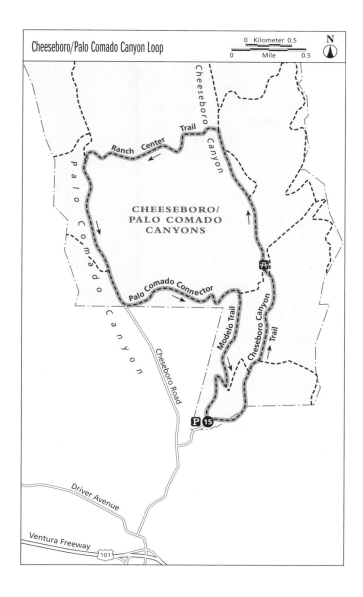

0   Kilometer   0.5

0   Mile   0.5

N

Cheeseboro Canyon

Ranch   Center   Trail

Palo   Comado   Canyon

CHEESEBORO/
PALO COMADO
CANYONS

Palo Comado Connector

Modelo Trail

Cheeseboro Canyon   Trail

P 15

Cheseboro Road

Driver Avenue

Ventura Freeway   101

3.4 Turn left onto the Palo Comado Canyon Trail. Stay on the main trail.

4.5 Turn left at the fork and intersection with Chesebro Road.

5.4 Turn right onto the Modelo Trail.

6.1 Turn right at the junction and follow the Modelo Trail back to the parking lot.

6.6 Arrive back at the trailhead.

16 **Solstice Canyon**

Hike through a beautiful canyon to the remains of two ruined mansions, and espy a lovely waterfall.

Distance: 3.1-mile loop
Approximate hiking time: 2 hours
Elevation gain: 1,000 feet
Difficulty: Easy
Trail surface: Dirt, rock, asphalt
Best season: Year-round; late winter and early spring for water and wildflowers
Other trail users: None

Canine compatibility: Leashed dogs permitted
Fees and permits: None
Trail contact: Santa Monica Mountains National Recreation Area, 401 West Hillcrest Dr., Thousand Oaks, CA 91360; (805) 370-2301; www.nps.gov/samo

Finding the trailhead: From the intersection of US 101 and Lindero Canyon Road in Westlake Village, head southeast on US 101 for 6.7 miles. Take exit 33 for Lost Hills Road. Drive 1.1 miles and turn right onto Las Virgenes Road/Malibu Canyon Road. Drive for 7.9 miles. Turn right onto CA 1/Pacific Coast Highway. Drive for 2.3 miles. Turn right onto Corral Canyon Road. Drive for 0.2 mile to the parking area. The trail is obvious, walk up the road beyond the restrooms. GPS Trailhead Coordinates: 34° 02' 15" N, -118° 44' 54" W

The Hike

Make no mistake, Solstice Canyon is remarkably beautiful and lush. There is no doubt that it is one of the best hikes in the Santa Monica Mountains National Recreation Area. However, seclusion and solitude are decidedly not on the itinerary. This is the most popular hike in Malibu and with good reason. There are several sets of ruins, including the

Keller House, which stood almost one hundred years, from 1903 until 2007, and the Roberts Ranch House, built in 1952 by architect Paul Williams.

The canyon is wide, lined with trees and foliage: Truly the place is overflowing with life. From the upper parking area, begin walking west up the roadway, which is the Solstice Canyon Trail. Stay on the pavement and follow it left at the first three junctions. At 0.35 mile, turn right and follow the road north along the main trail. The trail is always active with people, though not overly crowded. There will always be others hiking in and out, but the canyon still feels magical.

At 0.6 mile the Keller House sits across the creek. A bridge can be crossed for those looking to steal a closer look. The ruins are protected by a chain-link fence, since the house's destruction at the hands of the Corral Fire in 2007.

Continue walking north and at the trail split, hikers can choose to hike along the creek or stay on the main route and hike just above it. The two separate trails merge back into one a little ways up the trail. The riparian woodland foliage in the canyon is lovely, and has recovered quite well from the Corral Fire in 2007. There are still signs of the damage done, but fire is a way of life for the canyon and part of the natural ecology.

The trail continues north through the peaceful canyon to the amazing ruins at Roberts Ranch. The beauty of this ruin cannot be understated. The acclaimed architect used the natural lines of the canyon in the house design, and even what remains after the 1982 Dayton Canyon Fire is stunning. It feels like an innate piece of the landscape. Behind the ruin is the true wonder of the canyon, a two-tiered cascade that runs year-round. The waterfall, though small,

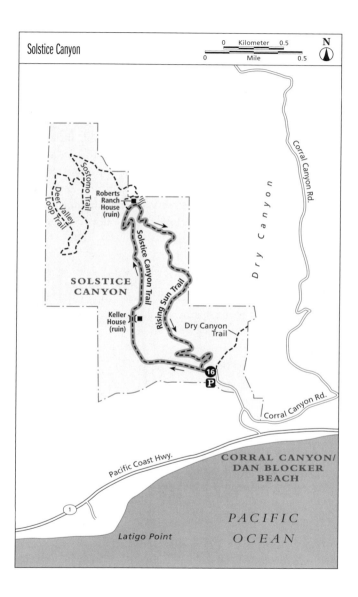

Solstice Canyon

0   Kilometer   0.5
0   Mile   0.5

N

Corral Canyon Rd.

Sostomo Trail

Deer Valley Loop Trail

Roberts Ranch House (ruin)

Solstice Canyon Trail

SOLSTICE CANYON

D r y   C a n y o n

Keller House (ruin)

Rising Sun Trail

Dry Canyon Trail

16
P

Corral Canyon Rd.

Pacific Coast Hwy.

1

CORRAL CANYON/
DAN BLOCKER
BEACH

Latigo Point

PACIFIC
OCEAN

is one of the most picturesque in all of Southern California. Enjoy the splendor.

Walk behind the ruins, following the creek to the signed Rising Sun Trail. Look for the shrine and statues just after crossing the creek. Most people overlook this cool little hidden temple. The Rising Sun Trail rises above the canyon and probably got its name because there is very little shade and morning is the best time to avoid the heat. This section of the trail is remarkably less used than the main route. It climbs up out of the canyon, gaining 400 feet of elevation in a little less than 0.25 mile. From here, the views of the Pacific and the canyon are noteworthy. It is calming and somewhat idyllic to stare at the cool blue ocean as the trail descends back to the trailhead and parking lot.

Miles and Directions

0.0 From the upper parking lot, stay left on the Solstice Canyon Trail past the first three intersections.

0.35 Turn left and follow the main trail north up the canyon.

0.6 Pass the Keller House ruins.

0.7 Take the right or left fork.

1.0 The forks merge back into one trail.

1.4 Reach the Roberts Ranch House. Explore the ruins, waterfall, and statuary. Cross the creek to the signed Rising Sun Trail.

1.8 Climb to the highest point on the trail.

3.0 Turn left onto the main road toward the parking lot.

3.1 Arrive back at the trailhead and the parking area.

17 Red Rock Canyon

Hike through a beautifully secluded volcanic canyon.

Distance: 3.5 miles out and back

Approximate hiking time: 2 hours

Elevation gain: 400 feet

Difficulty: Easy

Trail surface: Dirt, rock, asphalt

Best season: Year-round; hot in summer

Other trail users: Equestrians, bicyclists

Canine compatibility: Leashed dogs permitted

Fees and permits: None

Trail contact: Red Rock Canyon Park, 23601 West Red Rock Rd., Topanga, CA 90290; www.lamountains.com/parks .asp?parkid=47. Santa Monica Mountains National Recreation Area, 401 West Hillcrest Dr., Thousand Oaks, CA 91360; (805) 370-2301; www.nps.gov/ samo

Finding the trailhead: From the intersection of US 101 and Lindero Canyon Road in Westlake Village, head southeast on US 101 for 9.9 miles. Take exit 29 for Mulholland Drive/Valley Circle Boulevard. Turn left onto Calabasas Road, and drive for 0.1 mile. Turn right onto Mulholland Drive and drive for 0.5 mile. Turn right onto Valmar Road/Old Topanga Canyon Road and drive for 1.2 miles. Make a slight right onto Mulholland Highway and drive for 0.2 mile. Turn left onto Old Topanga Canyon Road and stay on Old Topanga Canyon Road for 3.9 miles. Turn right at Red Rock Road. Drive for 0.8 mile to the parking area signed for Red Rock Canyon. GPS Trailhead Coordinates: 34° 06' 20" N, -118° 38' 16" W

The Hike

From the parking lot at the end of the narrow dirt road, walk west past the picnic tables, ranger residence, and

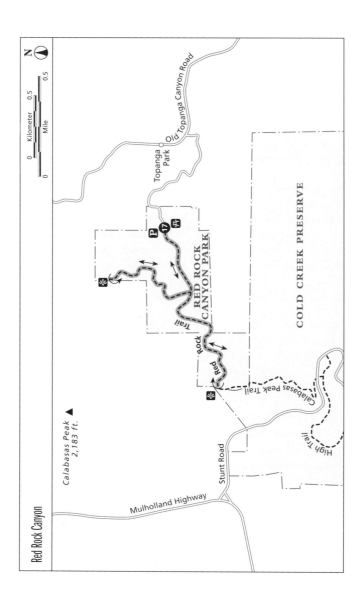

Red Rock Canyon

Calabasas Peak ▲
2,183 ft.

Mulholland Highway

Stunt Road

COLD CREEK PRESERVE

RED ROCK CANYON PARK

Red Rock Trail

Calabasas Peak Trail

High Trail

Topanga Park

Old Topanga Canyon Road

N

Kilometer   0.5
0   0.5
0   Mile   0.5

restrooms. At 0.3 mile, along an intermittent creek, formations of sandstone and red rock begin to appear. The small caves on the left are great for exploring. Those looking for adventure may want to climb around to get on top of the rocks for a nice view of the park and the strange formations. At the 0.35-mile mark, turn right, cross the creek, and walk north onto the unsigned trail. The trail climbs straight into the heart of the eerily exposed rock. Smooth, angled, jutting boulders stick straight out of the earth, some complete with arches and caves. The colors of the rocks run the spectrum from white to red to pink. Some are beautiful, most are odd, and the landscape feels quite unique for the region. The only thing that detracts from the park's beauty are the telephone lines that run straight along Red Rock Canyon Road.

The trail climbs 400 feet in elevation to an overlook at the 1-mile mark. Here, there are great views down into the canyon. Return back to the roadway, enjoying the change of perspective on the way back down the trail. Make sure to look for shells embedded in the ancient rock.

The trail intersects the road at 1.7 miles. Turn right and walk up Red Rock Canyon Road. Follow the road as it climbs 300 feet to an overlook into Malibu Creek State Park and Diamond X Ranch.

At 2.5 miles the route reaches the turnaround point. Those with lots of energy may wish to tackle Calabasas Peak by turning right, although this adds an additional 600 feet of elevation and 2 miles to the round-trip. The views are quite outstanding though.

Those looking to keep the hike relatively easy should turn around and follow the road 1 mile back to the trailhead and parking area.

Miles and Directions

0.0 From the parking area walk west along Red Rock Canyon Road.

0.35 Turn right at the unsigned trail and walk north.

1.0 Reach the overlook; turn around and retrace your steps to the road.

1.7 Turn right at the road.

2.5 Arrive at the Calabasas Peak Trail junction and the turn-around point.

3.5 Arrive back at the trailhead and parking area.

18 Temescal Canyon (Temescal Gateway Park)

Walk through a beautiful coastal canyon to a waterfall on this wonderful loop trail.

Distance: 3.2-mile lollipop
Approximate hiking time: 1.5 hours
Elevation gain: 900 feet
Difficulty: Easy
Trail surface: Dirt, pavement
Best season: Year-round; spring for water and wildflowers
Other trail users: None
Canine compatibility: Dogs are allowed in Temescal Gateway Park, but not in Topanga Canyon State Park.
Fees and permits: A day use fee is charged.

Trail contact: Temescal Gateway Park, 15601 Sunset Blvd., Pacific Palisades, CA 90272; (310) 454-1395; www.lamoun tains.com/parks.asp?parkid=58. Topanga Canyon State Park, 20829 Entrada Rd., Topanga, CA 90290; (310) 455-2465; www .parks.ca.gov/default.asp?page_ id=629. Santa Monica Mountains National Recreation Area, 401 West Hillcrest Dr., Thousand Oaks, CA 91360; (805) 370-2301; www.nps.gov/samo

Finding the trailhead: From the intersection of US 101 and Lindero Canyon Road in Westlake Village, head southeast on US 101 for 11.6 miles. Take exit 27 for Ventura Boulevard/Topanga Canyon Boulevard. Drive on Ventura Boulevard for 0.5 mile. Turn right onto CA 27/Topanga Canyon Boulevard. Drive for 12.2 miles. Turn left onto CA 1/Pacific Coast Highway. Drive for 2.6 miles. Turn left onto Temescal Canyon Road. Drive for 1.1 miles to the entrance of the park. Park in the lot. GPS Trailhead Coordinates: 34° 03' 04" N, -118° 31' 45" W

The Hike

A hike through Temescal Canyon is without a doubt lovely. Complete with views that border on sensory overload, a quaint series of waterfalls, and a busy but not overcrowded trail, there is something here for everyone. Climbing up the canyon is a good workout, but nothing too taxing. In fact, the 3.2-mile hike is short enough to be a daily training hike for those living in the area who are looking to maximize their fitness regimens, and hoping to take on longer hikes and significantly larger peaks.

In fact, the only negative things about the area are the rather draconian parking regulations and enforcement, fee restrictions, and photo-enforced stop signs. Make certain to follow every rule and to cross your t's and dot your i's: If you don't you may find a citation waiting on your dash even if you think you've done everything correctly. Read the fine print on this one, and stop completely at all of the stop signs.

From the first parking area, walk up Temescal Canyon Road. Follow the pavement beyond the store and rest-rooms. Continue for 0.3 mile. Go right next to some cabins, continuing to where the pavement eventually becomes a dirt trail. The trail continues past a couple of wooden support dams designed to hold back fast-moving earth in case of flooding and/or landslides, and eventually narrows to a wide singletrack trail. Heading up the eastern side of the loop first has the distinct advantage of staying in shade and under tree cover for most of the climb.

At 0.75 mile the trail begins to climb, gradually at first, and then ascending steeply to the lovely series of cascading waterfalls at 1.4 miles. A bridge crosses the creek just below

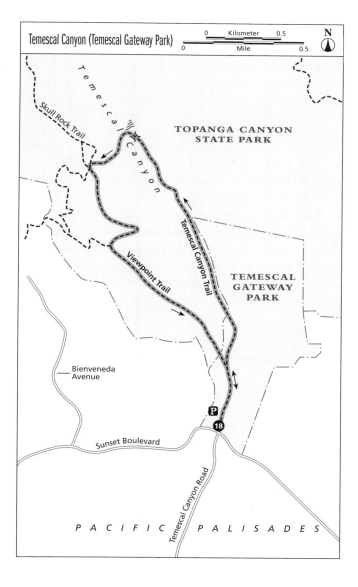

Temescal Canyon (Temescal Gateway Park)

Kilometer
0   0.5
Mile
0   0.5

N

Temescal Canyon

Skull Rock Trail

TOPANGA CANYON
STATE PARK

Temescal Canyon Trail

Viewpoint Trail

TEMESCAL
GATEWAY
PARK

Bienveneda
Avenue

P
18

Sunset Boulevard

Temescal Canyon Road

PACIFIC PALISADES

the smaller of the two cascades. The larger cascade sits just below the bridge. It isn't wise to descend down to the lower falls as the only use path is completely covered in poison oak. Visitors descending to the rather large pool and more picturesque falls may leave with more than they bargained for. Watch out for poison oak all along the trail.

After enjoying the waterfalls and babbling creek, continue over the footbridge and climb to the 1.6-mile mark. Stay left at the junction with the Skull Rock Trail. The trails are very well signed and it is easy to stay on the correct route. Continue for 0.1 mile, to where the views of Malibu and Santa Monica open up, as does the trail. Turn left again at the next junction and descend back to the parking area. There are intermittent patches of shade on the western side of the route, but the path is much more exposed to the sun. The descent is very gradual and leads right back to the roadway and trailhead.

Miles and Directions

0.0 From the parking area, walk north up paved Temescal Canyon Road.

0.3 Turn right at the Y intersection.

0.5 The road narrows to a dirt trail; continue north.

1.0 Enter Topanga Canyon State Park.

1.4 Arrive at the waterfall and footbridge.

1.6 Stay left at the junction with Skull Rock Trail.

1.7 Turn left at the junction.

2.7 Rejoin the road; walk south to the parking area.

3.2 Arrive at the trailhead and the parking area.

About the Author

Allen Riedel is a photographer, journalist, author, and teacher. He lives with his wife, Monique, and children, Michael, Sierra, and Makaila, in Riverside, California. He writes an outdoor column for the *Press Enterprise,* and has authored several hiking guides, including: *Best Hikes with Dogs in Southern California, 100 Classic Hikes in Southern California, Best Easy Day Hikes Riverside, Best Easy Day Hikes San Bernardino, Best Easy Day Hikes San Gabriel Valley, Best Easy Day Hikes San Diego, Best Easy Day Hikes South Bay,* and the upcoming *Best Easy Day Hikes San Luis Obispo.*

What's So Special about Unspoiled, Natural Places?

Beauty   Solitude   Wildness   Freedom   Quiet   Adventure
Serenity   Inspiration   Wonder   Excitement
Relaxation   Challenge

There's a lot to love about our treasured public lands, and the reasons are different for each of us. Whatever your reasons are, the national **Leave No Trace** education program will help you discover special outdoor places, enjoy them, and preserve them—today and for those who follow. By practicing and passing along these simple principles, you can help protect the special places you love from being loved to death.

The Principles of Leave No Trace

- Plan ahead and prepare
- Travel and camp on durable surfaces
- Dispose of waste properly
- Leave what you find
- Minimize campfire impacts
- Respect wildlife
- Be considerate of other visitors

Leave No Trace is a national nonprofit organization dedicated to teaching responsible outdoor recreation skills and ethics to everyone who enjoys spending time outdoors.

To learn more or to become a member, please visit us at www.LNT.org or call (800) 332-4100.

Leave No Trace, P.O. Box 997, Boulder, CO 80306